Successful Schools and Competent Students

James Garbarino
The Pennsylvania State
University

with the assistance of
C. Elliott Asp
The Pennsylvania State
University

LexingtonBooks
D.C. Heath and Company
Lexington, Massachusetts
Toronto

To Nan

Library of Congress Cataloging in Publication Data

Garbarino, James
 Successful schools and competent students.

 Includes index.
 1. Public schools—United States. 2. Prediction of scholastic success.
3. Academic achievement. I. Asp, C. Elliott. II. Title.
LA212.G29   370′.973   81-47004
ISBN 0-669-04526-8   AACR2

Copyright © 1981 by D.C. Heath and Company

Published simultaneously in Canada

Printed in the United States of America

International Standard Book Number: 0-669-04526-8

Library of Congress Catalog Card Number: 81-47004

Contents

Preface and Acknowledgments

This book presents a social and developmental perspective on schools and schooling. It seeks to develop a view of education that makes sense philosophically, scientifically, and politically—although some, no doubt, will find it philosophically, scientifically, and politically controversial. The book is an essay with a point of view rather than simply a review of the literature. My experiences as a teacher (at the elementary, secondary, and collegiate levels) and as a student of human development lead me to look beyond educational psychology and instructional technique to find criteria with which to evaluate U.S. education. This book tells what I found when I tried to make sense of the meaning and origins of school success.

As in any intellectual endeavor, there have been many collaborators. First among these is Elliott Asp, who assisted me in the final writing and technical preparation of the manuscript. His experiences as a teacher and his thoughtful suggestions enriched this book in many ways. Much of the work that went into this book took place while I was a Spencer Fellow with the support of the National Academy of Education, and their support did much to facilitate the mechanics of writing. I also have benefited from the institutional support offered, first, by Empire State College; then by the Boys Town Center for the Study of Youth Development; and, most recently, by the Department of Individual and Family Studies at The Pennsylvania State University, where I now make my intellectual home. Special thanks go to Alice Saxion for her secretarial (not to mention moral) support; to the typists who shouldered the burden of typing those seemingly endless revisions (Kathie Hooven, Joy Barger, and Sally Barber); and the many friends and colleagues who encouraged me along the way.

1

The Impossible School

The Context of Schools and Schooling

The 1970s were a difficult time for education in the United States. After the buoyant optimism of the 1960s, in which everything was promised on behalf of schools and schooling, the 1970s saw the appearance of what Godfrey Hodgson ominously labeled "the retreat from education."[1] In the affluent early years of the Great Society, with its declared goal of eradicating poverty and ignorance, the United States designated its schools as both the vehicles and the battlegrounds for the improvement of the human condition. The traditional dream of upward mobility through education reached its zenith in the 1960s. We were to fight racial injustice first through school desegregation and ultimately through integration of the schools. The culture of poverty was to be eliminated through programs of academic enrichment—at all age levels, starting with the nation's preschools and continuing through its colleges. Likewise, humanists and liberationists of all sorts looked to such concepts as "open education" and "free schools" for the fulfillment of their dreams.

These dreams have now lost much of their credibility in the minds of private citizens, researchers, educators, and politicians. The unrealistic optimism of the 1960s encouraged us, as a society, to believe that schools and schooling could do everything. The 1970s brought a backlash in which we were told that the schools could do little if anything to deliver on the dream of a Great Society. This public despair over the efficacy of education is linked, as both cause and effect, to the current state of research and theory on schools and schooling.

In many ways, our thinking about education in the United States has come to a standstill. The public's doubts and fears grow in a climate marked by disruption, violence, and apathy. Educators are beset by conflicting advice, recommendations, mandates, and demands from all quarters. The consensus necessary to sustain coherent and informed action is absent. Morale is low in schools across the country. Education is indeed in abscission, increasingly cut off from a firm theoretical base, from coherent social policy, and from a mutually satisfying relationship with its employees and clients.

How can we come to a coherent understanding of schools and schooling? We need a better understanding of the meaning, origins, and conse-

1

quences of school success in U.S. life. We can draw on, but must go beyond, existing reviews of educational psychology and of the sociology of education. We need to understand where school success fits into the fabric of life in the United States. Our definition of school success should be grounded in the day-to-day experience of social reality in its totality, not primarily in the grade books of teachers. "School success" means an assessment of the success of schools in relating to U.S. society as much as it does the achievement of individuals or groups in the classroom. We need an analysis rooted in an ecologically valid conception of education. Beginning with the current standstill in research and theory on education, we must arrive at a synthesis that will permit new forward movement. In so doing we can halt Hodgson's "retreat from education" and signal a new advance.

Fantasy Schools and Real People

Our fundamental problems are conceptual. Both the professional community and the society at large maintain an inadequate conception of the meaning and origins of school success. This faulty idea generates a series of intellectual problems that have compounded a set of difficulties involving the very social foundations of schools and schooling.

The overriding intellectual problem is that both major thrusts in educational research have been conceptually and methodologically inadequate to the demands of social and educational policy. One thrust consists of "small" studies and experiments, research that is often technically sophisticated but is typically ecologically invalid and socially naive. This emphasis has led to a plethora of "findings" but little insight into the basic phenomena of schools and schooling as they exist on a day-to-day basis. The second approach relies on massive analyses of the objective conditions of education in an attempt to define and isolate the unique contribution of each element to differences in academic achievement. These studies have often violated or ignored the social reality of schools and schooling. Moreover, on balance they have tended to create the impression in the minds of the public and of many members of the education business that no element matters very much. Whether or not this impression accurately reflects either the data or the investigator's intentions, it nonetheless seems to have occurred. And, as we all know, situations perceived as real tend to have real consequences.

The nature and scope of this twofold intellectual problem became apparent during the 1970s, as many researchers, from a variety of backgrounds, came up against the complex and difficult task of applying their knowledge about education to issues in the real world. This is true both at the micro level—as in the development of intervention programs, teaching machines, or alternative schools—and at the macro level—as in efforts to achieve desegregation and to mitigate the human devastation caused by poverty. The conclusions reached by investigators who have examined the usefulness of educational research and theory in meeting the needs of schools and society illustrates this problem.

For example, when Jonathan Stephens undertook a comprehensive review of the process of schooling, he was disappointed with the results.[2] Noting the thousands of studies dealing with educational effectiveness, he despaired over the little genuine progress that had been made: "Regarding the essential mechanisms of schooling, however, we even lack serious detailed speculation, to say nothing of convincing evidence."[3]

A Rand Corporation study (in many ways the most thorough of its kind) echoed this conclusion:

> The vast body of literature on educational effectiveness should provide a firm foundation for the formulation of educational policy. Thus far, it has not done so.[4]

In a critique of educational research related to the effects of desegregation, Robert Crain felt compelled to call the resulting paper, "Why Academic Research Fails to be Useful."[5] In it, he posed and then answered a critical policy question. Asking if research has helped to resolve the issue of school desegregation, he concluded that it has not. "A great deal has been written on school desegregation, but it has not been useful."[6] The volume of literature tells us very little of real practical value.

The dimensions of the problem of inadequate research on schools and schooling become evident when one examines specific issues such as computer-assisted instruction ("teaching machines"), the allocation of financial resources to improve schooling, classroom reform ("educational innovation"), or the role of schools in racial desegregation. The following examples will serve to identify the ways in which an inadequate research base contributes to problems in each of these areas.

Of computer-assisted instruction (CAI), one analyst, Lawrence Stolurow, has concluded that real advances await progress in formulating a comprehensive and validated theory of teaching.[7] He notes that "CAI makes our meager knowledge of teaching patently obvious. Our ignorance cannot go unnoticed as with some other forms of instruction."[8]

This view is shared by many who seriously consider the possibility of teaching machines—and should be by those who do not.[9] Moreover, the air of social and fiscal unreality surrounding much of what is written and said about technology-intensive education is astounding. With many teachers worried about getting through the day unmolested and most administrators worried about meeting the payroll for personnel and essential operating expenses, talk of widespread technological innovation seems like mere wishful thinking to be confined to pockets of affluence, to schools underwritten by universities and corporate-foundation seed money.

Of the problem of allocating financial resources to improve educational quality, a Rand Corporation study concluded that conventional patterns of investment offer little or no payoff in terms of student outcomes. The study reports, "Increasing expenditures on traditional educational practices is not likely to improve educational outcomes substantially."[10]

On the topic of classroom reform there has been much debate but little understanding. Support for this conclusion comes from many quarters. There appears to be a growing realization that the problem is a complex one, because the effectiveness of one aspect of schooling depends on its relationship to the context in which it occurs. The Rand Corporation study concluded that the match of student to technique is vitally important: "There may not be any *universally* effective educational practices."[11]

Much has been made of educational systems. The educational-research establishment has been drawn to systems theory as a conceptual model for understanding and rationally changing schools and schooling. As Oettinger made clear, however, our understanding of schools as systems is inadequate.[12] He sets forth the necessary conditions for a valid systems-theory application.

1. The system being studied must be sufficiently independent of the systems that combined with it to form a suprasystem, that interactions among these systems can be either satisfactorily accounted for or else ignored, without dire consequences.
2. The system being studied must be one for which well-developed and proved research and design tools exist.
3. When designing a system, we must know explicitly what it is for.[13]

According to Oettinger, among many others, education and our understanding of it do not meet these necessary conditions. Educational reforms burst forth, flower, die, and then are reborn—only to fail once more. The history of educational reform has been one of recurrent frustration, dating back to the seventeenth century, if not earlier. In his classic analysis of schooling, *The Great Didactic*, written in 1632, John Amos Comenius stated:

> For more than a hundred years much complaint has been made of the unmethodical way in which schools are conducted, but it is only within the last thirty that any serious attempt has been made to find a remedy for this state of things. And with what result? Schools remain exactly as they were.[14]

Stephens echoed this theme, not without some rancor, in his own analysis. Despite constant "innovations" which typically are in fact the innovations of an earlier generation, he said, "academic growth within the classroom continues at about the same rate, stubbornly refusing to co-operate with the bright new dicta emanating from the conference room."[15]

In his discussion of the "crisis in the classroom," Charles Silberman made much the same point: ". . . the reform movement has produced innumerable changes, and yet the schools themselves are largely unchanged."[16]

The middle-school movement of the 1960s is a case in point. Hailed as a program designed specifically for early adolescents, the middle school was conceived out of criticism of the discipline-bound, high-school-mimicking nature of the traditional junior high school. The middle school was to be a new educational entity that would replace the developmentally unsound junior high school. Thus, middle schools should bear little if any resemblance to traditional junior highs. However, in a 1978 survey of the state of the middle school, Brooks and Edwards noted that "the data presented in this document did not particularly point to a curriculum orientation uniquely different from other alternatives, such as traditional junior high schools."[17] At this point, middle schools appear to be simply another reform that has produced little change.

The 1970s provided many vivid reaffirmations of this theme. The history of John Adams High School, one of the most highly acclaimed efforts of the 1970s at educational innovation at the secondary level, is a poignant example. In his discussion of U.S. education in 1970, Silberman looked to the John Adams High School in Oregon, then new, as a promising sign.[18] Adams began with a great deal of fanfare, and much was both promised and expected on its behalf. It opened with a large infusion of educational expertise, including staff from the Harvard University School of Education. It had 1,650 students, 80 teachers, 80 trainees, and 30 paraprofessionals. In many ways the Adams project represented the best aspects of the standard U.S. paradigm of education and innovation, and in some sense it may represent the best we can do with the existing models. What were the results? At least at first, a large number of good students enjoyed the program and prospered in it. This, of course, is the case with any school that serves a substantial proportion of "good" students, those with the socioeconomic resources and background in the academic culture to succeed in U.S. schools. Trouble soon arose, however. The staff reported that the school was not working for many students, for those who

> have been damaged by previous failure or for other reasons, feel alienated from the entire process of schooling and have very little interest in assuming responsibility for their own learning, at least within the school.[19]

Moreover, despite the high hopes, and despite the unusual concentration of the "best and the brightest" for staff support, in 1971 a member of the Adams staff concluded that

> virtually everyone at Adams involved in instruction is in a state of near
> exhaustion. There is simply too much work to do with insufficient
> resources to accomplish it.[20]

By 1980 the picture was even bleaker. *Newsweek* published a report on
Adams, entitled "The School that Flunked."[21] The school that the Carnegie
Foundation had called possibly "the most important experiment in secondary education" seemed about to end, not with a bang but with a
whimper. Faced with student and parent dissatisfaction, the staff eventually
scrapped much of the innovative program in favor of more traditional
elements, elements that seemed better able to meet some of the basic
psychological needs of both students and staff. The elaborate abstractions
of the school's founders have given way to a more conventional model.

The real question raised by this case study is that, if Adams possessed
"insufficient resources," then what hope is there for less-well-endowed
schools (that is, most schools)? In the retrenchment economy of the 1980s
there is little prospect for increasing resources of the kind on which the
Adams project depended. The problem, the real crisis, is the inadequacy of
one basic resource—knowledge of how schools and schooling really work.
The school that existed in the minds of the creative people who designed
Adams High School is an impossibility, a fantasy school that exists only in
the minds and hearts of educational theorists and visionaries. In fact, there
is nothing so lethal to it as the flesh-and-blood teachers and students within
the walls of real schools, hence the desire often expressed by educational in-
novators to "teacher-proof" their creations. This impossible school is an
illustration of educational policy and practice fit only for the academic
hothouse—too frail for the grubby hands of teachers and students. Nevertheless, our society continues to look for educational panaceas.

The method by which we perpetuate such fantasies can be seen more
clearly in the way professional educationalists (as opposed to educators)
treat the experience of schooling by ordinary students and teachers. One
such record is found in a book edited by John Flanagan.[22] This book asks
the educationally noble question, "How can we draw upon the experiences
of former students and consequently evaluate the past performance of
schools and propose new directions for education?"[23] Flanagan and his colleagues sought to answer this question, with, at best, mixed results. They
based their work on Project Talent, a huge investigation of students, education, and the interaction of the two that was begun in the late 1950s and has
now culminated in a spate of longitudinal studies. In this book, ten experts
comment on the role of education in the life stories of a subset of the
students involved in Project Talent.

This book focuses on the consequences of education, as perceived by
former students. In a series of brief essays, the panel of experts offers com-

mentary on how well school worked for a group of students who were 15 in 1960. Looking back in 1975, these young people examine how they felt about schooling, their teachers, guidance, and the overall academic program. Further, they relate their views on how well schooling has served them and on how they see it fitting into and affecting their lives. Each panel expert closely reviewed narrative reports of 100 of the cases selected from the larger pool of 1,000 30-year-olds interviewed in 1975.

According to both the students and the experts, school did not work very well at all for these young people.

> One cannot conclude from the evidence examined that formal high school studies have contributed greatly to either the performance or to the satisfaction of life activities. . . . The broad effects of "general" education are at least obscure and may be absent.[24]

The experts' commentary does, of course, have its bright spots; there is some positive evaluation of schools and of secondary education in the United States. But even these positive comments often take the form of backhanded compliments. Most notably, schools earned relatively high marks from their former students in providing a social order at least as decent and humane as the rest of society. Often a student would recall some individual teacher who, through personal dedication and compassion, had had a positive effect on his or her life. Many also recalled, of course, teachers who had had a negative effect. Perhaps the best that can be said of schools is found in the essay by Ralph W. Tyler, who observed that schools did provide "the opportunity for students to learn to read, write, and compute and to discover and use the sources of facts, principles, and ideas."[25]

It would seem that, in the minds of the panel experts, fulfilling these two functions is not enough. The experts seem to demand more of the schools than simply decency and opportunity, and herein lies the problem. Yet it is no mean accomplishment to provide a socially decent situation in which to learn and grow up. Recent studies of the violence and disruption in schools in the 1970s point up the value of security and opportunity.[26]

The panel experts present a mixture of feelings in their review of the Project Talent students. On the one hand, many are appalled at the lack of interest in and attention to the "higher things in life" among this group of U.S. citizens. On the other hand, there is genuine sympathy for the distress experienced and reported by the Project Talent sample. This mix of feelings, a kind of approach—withdrawal syndrome, seems to be linked to a basic lack of clarity and realism about what is possible in U.S. society, of which school is but a microcosm.

An idealization of the educational process and its attendant counseling functions emerges in the experts' essay. Among the many reasons that the schools failed to reach pupils in ways that affected their personal adjustment, two stand out: (1) school counselors are inadequately trained to perform therapeutic functions or even effectively to pursue mental-illness prevention, and (2) the community does not endorse therapeutic goals for schools.[27] This glorification of guidance implies that it somehow can and will provide deliverance to children. There is a belief that education itself can deliver U.S. youth from what one of the experts calls "living a passive, dull existence, without creative or intellectual spark. The life is gray, alienated, and kindled only with the hope that things might be better for one's children."[28] Another of the experts believes the schools are characterized by "education for non-citizenship, or education for apathy."[29] These judgments are, of course, the stuff of which Adams High School was built.

American intellectuals have had a long and stormy affair with education. Few topics produce such heights of visionary ecstasy or such depths of indignant criticism. A colleague recalls two experiences as a young teacher in a junior high school. The first involved being told by a principal that he thought too much about his work and was making far too much of it intellectually. The principal suggested he go back to the university "where he belonged." The second incident involved being told (in education courses at the university) that teaching was a "sacred trust" to bring forth the creative human potential of each student. The instructor painted a picture of an intellectual nirvana awaiting the teacher in the classroom. These experiences are typical of education in the United States. Both are real, but neither tells the whole story. American education is neither a sow's ear nor a silk purse but, rather, a mixed bag.

Flanagan and his colleagues asked young adults, "What did you learn from high school?" They seemed to answer, "Very little." One is tempted to ask the same question of the experts. What did they learn from the data they reviewed? Like the students, they seem to have come away with what they brought to the experience. The evidence, like the experience of schooling, is reported and evaluated through the eyes of the beholder.[30]

In the field of alternative education our ignorance and impotence can lead to frustration and wasted resources. The problem becomes even more serious, however, when the issue is something as politically explosive as the role of the schools in the conjoint problems of race and social class. As was noted before, Crain's critique points to a serious failure in this regard. Our research models and the studies they generate are fundamentally invalid. Crain cited several reasons for this. The allocation of funding and the role of research in the careers of the investigators engenders small studies that are inadequate in scope and duration. The "culture of social science" impedes development of needed answers by downgrading applied research and severing the naturally symbiotic relationship between practical and theoretical knowledge.[31] Chase studied the value structure of social-science journals and found that, of ten evaluative criteria used to judge the merit of articles, "applicability to practical problems" ranked lowest in importance.[32] This split between "pure" and "applied" research is not confined to educational research, of course; it plagues developmental research of all types.[33] As the limitations of research results become apparent, the inadequacy of the model becomes clearer. In his introduction to Nancy St. John's *School Desegregation Outcomes for Children,* Nathan Glazer pinpoints the problem as it applies to the critical issue of racial desegregation by arguing that

> the overall inconclusiveness of the findings is due not so much to these [methodological] limitations as to the fallacious assumption that desegregation is a unitary variable, and that how it is implemented is of secondary importance.[34]

In matters of educational research and policy, it seems, *nothing* is a unitary variable. An understanding of the interaction of context and behavior is essential to all meaning and importance. The fundamental ecological invalidity of much of our research and theory on the process of schools and schooling poses a major intellectual problem. Moreover, this intellectual problem is particularly dangerous at this time in history because it hampers our ability to deal constructively and realistically with the many social problems that swirl in and around our schools.

Schools and Schooling

Does education in the United States face a crisis? In recent years, events have too often been exaggerated and sensationalized through the use of compelling prose. To be responsible we must be cautious. Silberman, for example, was careful to justify his assertion that the United States faced a "crisis in the classroom."[35] Silberman's crisis focused mainly on the climate and mechanics of teacher-student interaction. However, the crisis in U.S. education is best understood in the context of the crisis outside the classroom—in the halls, on the way to school, in the teachers' room, in the principal's office, in the board of education, and in educational research. The real crisis lies in the eroded foundations of U.S. education.

What is the mission of U.S. education? The collectivist nations such as China and the Soviet Union, as well as the Western European countries, emphasize education as character development in addition to academic achievement. In the United States, on the other hand, the emphasis is almost exclusively on so-called value-free academic achievement.[36] This narrowness, presumably born of our traditional separation of church and state and our assumption that moral training and character development are the rightful province of the family, has increased. This is paradoxical: During a time when the social role of schooling has *increased* (in granting social status, economic credentials, and so forth), the freeing of children from the authority and domination of traditional education has tended to *decrease* the overt role of schools as *deliberate* agents of socialization. After reviewing evidence on the role of schools in the process of social development, Heath concluded that the problem lies in a misunderstanding of what children need.

> Our singular pursuit of academic excellence, defined by narrow academic considerations, may have improved the academic preparation of some students but also have narrowed their sense of competence, limited their self-esteem, and made increasing numbers of them closed to subsequent intellectual growth.[37]

We must always remember that the school is usually the first social system that children encounter. In fact, it may be the only social system, other than the family, that they know well at all. We must therefore be very attentive to its structure and behavior as a context for socialization. We need to know where it fits into the overall human ecology and how it functions as a setting for child and youth development. To know where and how it fits into that human ecology, we must know what is required of children and youth as they mature and eventually make the transition to adulthood.[38] As Inkeles has made clear, we must know where children and youth are going if we are to assess the role that institutions like schools can play in enhancing or impeding their developmental process.[39] In general terms we need only recall Emile Durkheim's classic statement of the purposes of education.

> Education is the influence exercised by adult generations on those that are not yet ready for social life. Its object is to arouse and to develop in the child a certain number of physical, intellectual and moral states which are demanded of him by both the political society as a whole and the special milieu for which he is specifically destined.[40]

We owe our first allegiance as educators to this broad and grand mission.

The Social Context of Schools in the 1980s

Declining Academic Competence

Much has been made of the nationwide decline in Scholastic Aptitude Test (SAT) scores that has been observed ever since the scores reached their zenith in 1963. Between 1963 and 1980 mathematics scores dropped 36 points and verbal scores 54 points (from 502 to 466 and from 478 to 424, respectively, out of a possible total of 800 points on each test). Many explanations have been offered to account for this decline, which parallels declines in other indexes of academic competence, both formal and informal, systematic and anecdotal. Colleges report substantially decreased literary competence among entering students. Students' ability to express themselves in written form is often substandard compared with that of previous generations, according to the colleges. For example, the colleges of the University of California report that some 50 percent of entering students need substantial development of writing skills to meet minimal criteria of competence. This report echoes throughout the country. The skills of literacy appear to be declining among the supposedly educated.

Other data on academic development have raised the level of concern. The National Assessment of Educational Progress reported that a national comparison of science-achievement scores revealed a decline in competence between the late 1960s and the 1970s.[41] A study by the Department of Health, Education, and Welfare (DHEW) reported a decline in reading scores on a national basis that paralleled the SAT-score decrease.[42] A study in New York State likewise reported that "more and more children are below minimum competence" in reading each year.[43] As might be expected, the extent of these problems varies appreciably from place to place and from one socioeconomic group to another. Although it is a national phenomenon, affecting all areas, it is concentrated most heavily in isolated poor areas, both rural and urban. For example, Goldberg reports that the percentage of the ninth-grade students one or more grade levels behind in reading (that is, functionally illiterate) was 70 percent in the socioeconomically impoverished areas of New York City, compared with 21 percent in the other areas of the city.[44] However, the problem of incompetence appears to be increasing across social groups.[45] From graffiti to term papers, literary and arithmetic skills are appalling.

We should bear in mind that the mid-1960s represented in many ways the zenith of U.S. social history, the peak of the post-World War II socioeconomic blossoming that brought unprecedented affluence and educational development to a broad cross-section of U.S. citizens. "Until better evidence is presented, the tentative judgment must be that American children in the sixties are learning more than their older brothers and sisters learned in the fifties."[46] Silberman correctly noted that schools changed substantially in the postwar period and, by the mid-1960s, were doing a better job of educating minority-group and lower-class children than had the schools of a generation earlier.[47] This trend continued until the arrival of the retrenchment economy of the 1970s, which burst the bubble of progressivism and social development born of affluence. In a period of socioeconomic retrenchment, the stresses embedded in the social structure of U.S. life became manifest.

It is politically, morally, and intellectually important to recognize that the subsequent "failure" of U.S. education was not newly created in the

1960s and 1970s. It was, rather, the result of increased stress, in combination with declining support systems. As Silberman cautioned in 1970 (when the trends noted here were not yet widely publicized nor even clearly evident): "few things are more irritating than the mindless insistence that our problems represent a fall from some prior state of grace that never existed except in the critic's romantic imaginings."[48] It is important to remember that

> what we see as failure is not necessarily failure in any objective sense (there is little evidence, for example, that schools are any less successful now than they were in the past in transmitting basic skills to students), but failure relative to our heightened expectations for what schools can do.[49]

This caution should not be ignored, lest we too readily "cry wolf." At the same time, however, we cannot ignore the declining idexes of academic competence because in the present social context, in which academic success has become vital for socioeconomic success, academic competence is an important index of the quality of life. We demand a modicum of academic success as almost a precondition for full participation in the society.

Declining Standards of Social Conduct

All forms of delinquent behavior within the schools—vandalism, violence, and truancy—have increased. Unlike the workplace, the school is constantly threatened with indiscipline. Maintaining order has become a problem in schools, where rebellion and flouting of rules is the most common form of "worker alienation."[50]

Both objective and subjective evidence point to this problem. The annual "Poll of Public Attitudes Toward Education" conducted by the George Gallup organization has revealed that approximately one-quarter of the people of the United States believe that "lack of discipline" is the most important problem facing the public schools in their area.[51] Overall, lack of discipline is mentioned most often by respondents. This has been true for ten years of the eleven-year history (since 1969) of this annual poll. Perhaps more ominously, the 1975 report indicated a new concern: The number of respondents mentioning "crime" (vandalism, stealing, and so forth) was great enough to place this problem among the top ten.[52] Further evidence of trouble comes from the finding that, given the choice, 57 percent of the respondents would send their children "to a special public school that has strict discipline, including a dress code, and that puts emphasis on the three Rs."[53] Furthermore, most parents (79 percent in 1980) believe that the schools should engage in instruction dealing with morals and moral behavior.[54] This may be taken as evidence that people are becoming increasingly concerned about the moral climate both of the schools and of the society at large.

Other, more nearly "objective" data support these beliefs and perceptions. A report filed with the U.S. Senate indicates that in 1974 there were at least 70,000 serious assaults on teachers in U.S. schools and that $500 million worth of damage was done by vandals.[55] It was reported that 28 percent of all schools experience at least one act of vandalism a month (at an average cost of $81 per incident).[56] Whereas in 1966 U.S. schools employed only twenty-five people as "security guards," by 1976 some 25,000 people were so employed. Victimization (robbery, extortion, assault, and so forth) has become increasingly prevalent in schools throughout the country.[57] In a report compiled for the U.S. Department of Health, Education, and Welfare, it was stated that 50 percent of all assaults on 12- to 15-year-olds occur in schools and that 33 percent of all large-city junior-high-school students report being afraid to enter three or more areas within their schools.[58]

Students are not the only ones affected by school violence. A poll of teachers conducted by the National Education Association (NEA) revealed that, during the 1978-1979 school year, one out of every twenty teachers (a total of 110,000) was assaulted by students on school grounds, and that another 10,000 were attacked by students out of school. This was a 57 percent increase from the previous year. The poll also showed that 10 percent of all respondents were afraid of being attacked while in school, and 25 percent reported that they had had personal property stolen and/or damaged at school.[59]

Increased Alienation from Schools and Schooling

There is a growing gap between the conception of schools and schooling held by most adults and the experience of the students themselves. A 1972 study of a national sample of high-school seniors found that in response to the question, "How much has each of the following interfered with your education at this school?" nearly 40 percent said that "don't feel part of school" had interfered "somewhat" or "a great deal."[60] Differences in the ways that individuals and groups understand the reality of "shared" experiences can contribute significantly to important patterns of behavior. The conflict between what may be obvious to one party, but inconceivable to another, has a bearing on the kinds of solutions each sees as appropriate—if, indeed, there is even any agreement concerning the existence of a problem to be solved. It seems that significantly different conceptions of social reality exist to an ever increasing degree in the schools, particularly the secondary schools.

The New York State Commission on Quality, Cost and Financing of Elementary and Secondary Education (the Fleischmann commission) reported some information bearing on this question. For example:

In a New York State survey, 60 percent of the students indicated that they did not enjoy school.

When asked to rate school morale as "positive," "average," or "negative," 52 percent of the students picked "negative," whereas 64 percent of the teachers picked "positive."

When asked to rate the overall educational process on the same scale (that is, positive-average-negative) 52 percent of the teachers picked "positive," compared with 28 percent of the students.[61]

Such findings are a kind of prima facie evidence of alienation. Even allowing for some degree of negative exaggeration by students and positive exaggeration by teachers, the data indicate a serious lack of consensus between students and teachers regarding the day-to-day experience of education. Another New York State commission concluded that there has been a significant decline in morale and school spirit.[62]

Where there are not programs of school activities, the young people in this age group, in looking for something to do, often drift into antisocial behavior.[63]

One direct, simple index of alienation is attendance. In the schools hardest hit by social disruption, normal absence reaches nearly 50 percent.[64]

The problem of alienation, then, does seem to be of crisis dimensions, since it claims a major (and growing) percentage of adolescent students and is linked to asocial and antisocial behavior. Heath reports a growing trend toward social isolationism among middle-class students over the past twenty years or so.[65] Bronfenbrenner sees a pattern of social alienation.[66] Mackey detects a rise in "personal incapacity."[67] Heath found that whereas in 1948 only 33 percent of his students agreed with the statement, "When I was a child I didn't care to be a member of a crowd or group," by 1968 some 47 percent did. Likewise, in 1948, 23 percent said, "I could be happy living in a cabin in the woods or mountains"; but in 1968, 45 percent agreed with this statement. In 1948, 77 percent described themselves as "good mixers," as opposed to 43 percent in 1968.[68]

A Growing Problem of Morale

There seems to have been a decline in morale. Many believe that a cheapening of the role of teacher and labor disputes resulting in teacher strikes and

staff-community confrontation have fed this decline. The funding difficulties of many school districts compound these problems (according to a
1980 poll, 62 percent of school professionals felt that funding difficulties
were the biggest problem facing the schools today).[69] However, most morale
problems seem to stem from the amount of stress involved in teaching itself.
In fact, a favorite topic in many professional journals is how to deal with
the stresses and strains that are seemingly inherent in today's classrooms.
That teachers have had enough of this seems apparent. In both 1965 and
1971, a nationwide survey asked teachers to respond to the following question, "In general, how would you compare teaching as a profession today
and five years ago?" In 1965, 70.2 percent replied that teaching was getting
better. In 1971 only 34 percent said that it was getting better. On the other
hand, whereas in 1965, 13.1 percent said, "getting worse," in 1971, 29.6
percent gave that response.[70] (There has also been a marked decline in the
percentage of parents who would like their child to choose teaching as a
career.)[71] Fully 26 percent of the teachers responding in 1965 were no longer
teaching in 1971. By 1979 the situation had apparently deteriorated even
further. According to the NEA, one-third of those teaching in 1979 would
not choose to do so if they could go back to college and start over. The NEA
noted that only six out of ten teachers planned to stay until retirement and
that the number of teachers with twenty years or more of experience has
dropped by half in the past fifteen years.[72] We can ask for no clearer indication that teachers are frustrated with teaching and looking for a way out.[73]

The 1980 Gallup Poll of Public Attitudes Toward Education reports on
the grades given to schools. Since 1974 there has been a decline in the ratings
given to schools by the public, although in 1980 there was a slight increase in
the percentage of respondents giving the schools a grade of A. However, the
general trend has been downward, and the increase in As was accompanied
by a decrease in the number of Bs and an increase in the number of Ds.[74]

The public's rating of the schools may be influenced by the general loss
of confidence in and respect for all U.S. institutions. It should be pointed
out that education and the church still have much higher confidence ratings
than do Congress, the Supreme Court, organized labor, or big business,
however. A 1980 Gallup poll showed that the public gave a higher confidence rating (42 percent) to the schools than to local, state, and national
government (19 percent, 17 percent, and 14 percent), organized labor (17
percent), and big business (13 percent).[75] This level of confidence, then, is
something to build on. However, if it continues to slip, it will mean a profound social crisis for education as schools become even more dependent on
voluntary, interested support.

Another aspect of declining morale and evaluation is the growing view
that schools do not demand enough of students. This is a long-standing
view among high-school principals. As early as 1958, 90 percent of the

principals said that they thought schools demanded too little work from students.[76] The 1980 Gallup poll cited earlier shows that a large proportion of the general public has adopted this view. The question was directed at both elementary and secondary schools: "Do schools demand enough of students?" A majority responded that they do not believe that schools demand enough. The irony of all this does not escape many teachers, who blame education's current problems on "lack of support from the home." Indeed, in that same 1980 poll, professional educators listed lack of parental support as a major problem.[77] Many schools are plagued by charges and countercharges of this sort.

The Issue Is Human Quality

Our society faces a broad range of difficulties affecting children and youth. These problems cluster around the declining habitability of the social environment. They include child maltreatment, adolescent alcoholism, delinquency of all kinds, a generally decreased level of parental involvement, and a general lack of social identity. The root of these problems lies in forces that conspire against families, impairing their functioning and wrenching apart the bonds that bind adults and youth together in the social fabric of day-to-day experience.

At issue is the ability of families to function as educators. Basically, there are two ways in which families accomplish this role. First, families exhibit an "operational definition" of social reality. They provide a basis on which children can learn about human relations by directly or vicariously experiencing love, reason, anger, language, power, and the other primary aspects of being a person. These constitute the currency of the day-to-day behavior of human beings in families. In this way, one becomes a "chip off the old block." This process of *modeling* is crucial because it literally defines social reality for the child. Research has persuasively documented this effect in myriad ways, from the development of speech patterns to the use of physical force in influencing behavior.[78] Most theories of personality development, from social-learning theory to transactional analysis, recognize this. Second, in addition to modeling human relations, families *directly shape the learning of the child* by initiating and maintaining—or failing to initiate and maintain—developmentally enhancing relationships. These relationships teach important cognitive and affective skills and foster the development of prosocial values and characteristics. This process, known as *interaction style,* is a powerful one. For example, when parents enhance intelligence by promoting the child's use of language as a formal problem-solving mechanism, they also thereby provide a basis for subsequent academic learning.[79] By establishing strong attachment bonds between parents and children in the early months and years of life, families provide a basis for later social influence by nonparental adults. This social responsiveness is the source of the "social magnetism" that holds together the day-to-day life of the human community, and that makes human behavior humane.[80]

To be concerned with families and educators is to be interested in the forces that influence the operation and outcome of these two processes, modeling and interaction style. These forces are the variables of interest in a sound analysis of families as educators. The first is the degree to which families can and do model socially representative and valued patterns of behavior in their enduring relationships. Stability is crucial to the process of effective modeling. Thus an important issue is whether or not the family presents the child with an enduring social reality, particularly (1) enduring caregiving relationships, (2) enduring kinship relationships, and (3) enduring neighborhood relationships.

Enduring relationships have the potential to teach different things than do short-term relationships. Long-term relationships provide a greater potential for prosocial influence.[81] Enduring relationships enhance the power of the model and affect the degree to which the child is motivated to attend and is able to learn the subleties of the behavior or relationship in question, such as what it means to be a friend or a good worker. Families are effective as models and teachers of interactional style because they are so comprehensive and enduring; weakening this aspect of families reduces their power. We worry that American families are becoming weaker, and we wonder how the schools can help.

A second issue is the competence and health of the participants in families. Competence and health affect the ability and inclination of families to provide adequate models of successful and legitimate behavior patterns. We worry about the social and psychological resources of families—whether or not these are adequate to meet their obligations. In social terms, the issue is the balance between stresses and supports. Common stresses facing a family include excessive mobility, difficult commuting arrangements, lack of assistance in caregiving, racial discrimination, low socioeconomic status, and an unsupportive or hostile social environment. Family supports include availability of time for parenting and access to social services, friends, and relatives. In psychological terms, the critical factor is the adequacy of coping skills and a strong belief in personal accountability and self-determination. There is no substitute for the ability to persevere in the face of adversity, for the moral commitment to prosocial behavior, or for altruism. These are all components of what we commonly call "character," and can be contrasted to a pattern of pathological personality, behavior, and/or ideology characteristic of the chronically disorganized, incompetent, and generally unhealthy family. The match of family supports to stresses is, of course, the key.[82] Some families have great strength and resilience and may even appear invulnerable, whereas others appear weak and incapable of dealing with even moderate amounts of stress. However, a rising level of stress coupled with a decline in supports endangers normal families; and the early failure of the weak is only a precursor to more generalized problems. Some observers see this pattern in our recent history.

Stability and competence are the two factors that provide the context for families as educators. Where the social base of families is limited, their modeling capability is reduced. Pathological deviance or weakness diminishes the ability of families to generate and maintain developmentally enhancing relationships. Because in the United States families are the major repository of social authority and responsibility in matters of childhood socialization, the quality of family life bears a strong relationship to development of children. Making the environments in which families live more habitable is the best way to enhance the quality of life in our society.

This analysis places the ability of families to function in educative roles squarely within a social context. This aspect of family life cannot be understood unless we simultaneously consider the social factors that establish that context, thereby giving significance to each feature of family composition, organization, and behavior.

To understand the context in which families as educators must operate, we begin with a brief historical account of the status and composition of U.S. families in the post-World War II era. As we are all aware, this period has been one of change in the traditional structure of U.S. life.

Since World War II there have been discernible and widespread changes in the day-to-day composition of U.S. families, changes that have considerably reduced the social field for children and adults. There is an increasing likelihood that a child will grow up in a very small family (with only one adult and perhaps one other child). The increasing rate of single-parent families, one-child families, and families without any nonparental adult has tended to narrow the operational definition of American families. The census bureau estimates that roughly half of the children born in the United States in 1980 will spend some part of their first eighteen years in a single-parent household.[83]

Coupled with and exacerbating these changes in family composition is a generalized uprooting of families from enduring social contexts. Perhaps more important than the small size of many U.S. families is their lack of enduring relationships with neighbors and kin on a day-to-day basis. This narrows the basis on which children can learn through modeling. The lack of enduring relationships can impede a wide range of important emotional and intellectual developments among children. One of these problems may be the difficulty of teaching social identity without any enduring social context other than the socially small family. How can children develop a strong identity when they have little of an enduring nature with which to identify? Social identity comes from and along with a sense of community. U.S. families are increasingly communityless, frequently changing residences and/or living in noncommunities, places that do not possess the full range of human social life including commerce, age integration, kin, and other formal and informal institutions. The prime example of a noncommunity is the suburban "bedroom" housing development.[84]

The increase in pressures on families in the United States has made it ever more difficult for families to have the sustained concentration necessary to teach children how to be complete persons. Adults spend less time with children. The distractions of adult life—travel, career, "self-improvement"—seem to pull parents away from their children. Families are at root very conservative institutions, which make heavy demands for conservative virtues in adults, calling them to duty rather than mere pleasure.[85] The children of the United States are increasingly in settings dominated by autonomous peer groups, whose values often stand in stark contrast to the norms of families as educators. Peer groups divorced from the adult world are likely to promote asocial and even antisocial behavior. Moreover, children's contacts with nonparental adults increasingly tend to be impersonal and instrumental, as families are more often located in large, impersonal social settings that greatly inhibit reciprocal and enduring relationships of all kinds.

The educational task facing U.S. families have become more complex and more difficult. The increased importance of school success in shaping life outcomes has meant greater pressure on families to offer children the fundamentals of the academic culture—the web of abilities and values that underlies academic competence. Many families are not, and never have been, in a good position to do this. Increased flexibility of sex-role stereotypes increases the difficulty of "teaching" (let alone modeling) appropriate operational definitions of femininity and masculinity. The great demands on adults to deal with high levels of stress in the role of parent has made education within the family more problematic, a state that severely tries the resources of many families. Being a complete person is a more difficult task than it was, and it is likely to become still more difficult in the future as expectations and demands increase. Families as educators must be made up of "complete" human beings if they are to be successful.[86]

Conclusions

This chapter began with the proposition that U.S. education in the 1980s is in a muddle. It is cut off from a sound theoretical and empirical base, and this is an intellectual problem of major dimensions. Associated with this intellectual problem is the loss of faith in U.S. schools and schooling that Hodgson has called the "retreat from education." Professionals and the public alike are questioning the efficacy of the practice and institutions of education. These challenges are occurring in the midst of a pattern of social disturbance that in many respects deserves to be called a crisis. This is the intellectual, social, and historical context in which we seek to understand school success—its meaning, origins, and consequences. These contextual factors will be with us throughout our discussion, providing the discipline necessary to maintain the social validity and moral integrity of this analysis.

Notes

1. G. Hodgson, "Do Schools Make a Difference?" *Atlantic* 231 (1973):35-36.

2. J. Stephens, *The Process of Schooling: A Psychological Examination* (New York: Holt, Rinehart and Winston, 1967).

3. Ibid., p. 4.

4. H. Averch et al., *How Effective Is Schooling? A Critical Review of Research* (Englewood Cliffs, N.J.: Educational Technology Publications, 1974).

5. R. Crain, "Why Academic Research Fails to be Useful," *School Review* 84 (1976):337-351.

6. Ibid., p. 31.

7. L. Stolurow, *Computer-Assisted Instruction* (Detroit, Mich.: American Data Processing, Inc., 1968).

8. Ibid.

9. A. Oettinger, *Run Computer Run* (Cambridge, Mass.: Harvard University Press, 1969).

10. Averch, *How Effective Is Schooling?,* pp. 172-173.

11. Ibid., p. 173.

12. Oettinger, *Run Computer Run.*

13. Ibid., p. 55.

14. J. Comenius, *John Amos Comenius on Education* (New York: Teachers College Press, 1967).

15. Stephens, *The Process of Schooling,* p. 9.

16. C. Silberman, *Crisis in the Classroom: The Remaking of American Education* (New York: Random House, 1970).

17. K. Brooks and F. Edwards, "The Middle School in Transition," *CPD Memorandum,* Center for Professional Development, College of Education, University of Kentucky, 1978.

18. Silberman, *Crisis in the Classroom.*

19. A. Dobbins, "Instruction at Adams," *Phi Delta Kappan* 52 (1971):516-519.

20. Ibid., p. 519.

21. J. Adler and P. Abramson, "The School that Flunked," *Newsweek,* 6 October 1980, p. 86.

22. J. Flanagan, ed., *Perpectives on Improving Education: Project Talent's Young Adults Look Back* (New York: Praeger, 1978).

23. Ibid., p. 6.

24. Ibid., p. 35.

25. Ibid., p. 41.

26. U.S. Senate Subcommittee on the Judiciary, *Our Nation's Schools—A Report Card: "A" in School Violence and Vandalism.* Preliminary Report of the Subcommittee to Investigate Juvenile Delinquency, Committee Print, 94th Congress, 1st session. Washington, D.C.: U.S. Government Printing Office, 1975; *Violent Schools—Safe Schools: The Safe Schools Study Report to Congress.* U.S. Department of Health, Education, and Welfare. Washington, D.C.: U.S. Government Printing Office, 1977; K. Baker and R. Rubel, eds., *Violence and Crime in the Schools* (Lexington, Mass.: Lexington Books, D.C. Heath and Company, 1980).

27. Flanagan, *Project Talent,* p. 71.

28. Ibid., p. 69.

29. Ibid.

30. J. Garbarino, review of *Perspectives on Improving Education: Project Talent's Young Adults Look Back,* ed. J. Flanagan, *Children and Youth Services Review* 1 (1979):253-256.

31. Crain, "Academic Research," p. 342.

32. J. Chase, "Normative Criteria for Scientific Publication," *American Sociologist* 5 (1970):262-265.

33. J. Garbarino and U. Bronfenbrenner, *Research on Parent-Child Relations and Social Policy: How to Proceed,* Boys Town Center for the Study of Youth Development Working Paper Series, no. 1, 1977.

34. N. St. John, *School Desegregation Outcomes for Children* (New York: John Wiley and Sons, 1975).

35. Silberman, *Crisis in the Classroom.*

36. U. Bronfenbrenner, *Two Worlds of Childhood: U.S. and U.S.S.R.* (New York: Russell Sage Foundation, 1970).

37. D. Heath, "Student Alienation and School," *School Review* 78 (1970):515-528.

38. J. Garbarino, "The Role of Schools in Socialization to Adulthood," *Educational Forum* 42 (1978):169-182.

39. A. Inkeles, "Social Structure and the Organization of Competence," *Harvard Educational Review* 36 (1966):282.

40. E. Durkheim, *Education and Sociology* (New York: Free Press, 1956), p. 55.

41. National Center for Educational Statistics (NCES), *The Condition of Education: A Statistical Report on the Condition of American Education* (Washington, D.C.: U.S. Government Printing Office, 1975).

42. U. Bronfenbrenner, "The Origins of Alienation," in *Influences on Human Development*, ed. U. Bronfenbrenner and M. Mahoney (Hinsdale, Ill.: Dryden Press, 1975).

43. New York State Commission on the Quality, Cost, and Financing of Elementary and Secondary Education, *Final Report,* vols. 1-3 (Albany: State University of New York, State Education Department, 1972).

44. M. Goldberg, "Socio-Psychological Issues in the Education of the Disadvantaged," in *Urban Education in the 1970's,* ed. A. Parsons (New York: Columbia University Press, 1971), pp. 61-93.

45. Bronfenbrenner, "The Origins of Alienation."

46. U.S. Department of Health, Education and Welfare, *Toward a Social Report* (Washington, D.C.: U.S. Government Printing Office, 1969).

47. Silberman, *Crisis in the Classroom,* p. 162.

48. Ibid., p. 21.

49. C. Hurn, *The Limits and Possibilities of Schooling—An Introduction to the Sociology of Education* (Boston: Allyn and Bacon, 1978) p. 14.

50. A. Stinchcombe, *Rebellion in a High School* (Chicago: Quadrangle Books, 1964).

51. G. Gallup, "12th Annual Gallup Poll of the Public's Attitude Towards the Public Schools," *Phi Delta Kappan* 62 (1980):33-46.

52. G. Gallup, "The Public Looks at Education," *Today's Education* 64 (1975):16-20.

53. Ibid., p. 231.

54. Gallup, "12th Annual Poll," p. 39.

55. U.S. Senate Subcommittee on the Judiciary, *Our Nation's Schools.*

56. Baker and Rubel, *Crime in the Schools.*

57. J. Ban and L. Ciminillo, *Violence and Vandalism in Public Education* (Danville, Ill.: Interstate Printers and Publishers, Inc., 1977).

58. Baker and Rubel, *Crime in the Schools.*

59. National Education Association, "1979 Teachers Poll," *Today's Education* 68 (1979):10.

60. NCES, *The Condition of Education.*

61. New York State Commission on Quality, Cost and Financing of Elementary and Secondary Education, *Final Report.*

62. New York State Temporary Commission to Study the Causes of Campus Unrest, "The Academy in Turmoil: First Report," Albany, 1970; "Anarchy in the Academy: Second Report," Albany, 1971; "Academy or Battleground: Third Report," Albany, 1972.

63. Ibid., report no. 2, pp. 26-27.

64. Ibid., report no. 2, p. 40.

65. Heath, "Student Alienation and School."

66. Bronfenbrenner, "The Origins of Alienation."

67. J. Mackey, "Youth Alienation in Post-Modern Society," *The High School Journal* 61 (1978):353-367.

68. Heath, "Student Alienation and School."

69. S. Elam and P. Gough, "Comparing Lay and Professional Opinion on Gallup Poll Questions," *Phi Delta Kappan* 62 (1980):47-48.

70. Silberman, *Crisis in the Classroom.*

71. Gallup, "12th Annual Poll."

72. National Education Association, "1979 Teachers Poll."

73. Ibid.

74. Gallup, "12th Annual Poll."

75. Ibid.

76. R. Turner, *The Social Context of Ambition* (San Francisco: Chandler Publishing Company, 1964).

77. Gallup, "12th Annual Poll."

78. E.Schaefer, "Parents as Educators: Evidence from Cross-Sectional, Longitudinal, and Intervention Research," in *The Young Child,* vol. II, ed. W. Hartup (Washington, D.C.: National Association for the Education of Young Children, 1972).

79. U. Bronfenbrenner, *Is Early Intervention Effective?* (Washington, D.C.: U.S. Department of Health, Education, and Welfare, 1974).

80. J. Garbarino and U. Bronfenbrenner, "The Socialization of Moral Judgment and Behavior in Cross-Cultural Perspective," in *Moral Development and Behavior,* ed. T. Lickona (New York: Holt, Rinehart and Winston, 1976).

81. R. Barker and P. Gump, *Big School, Small School, High School Size and Student Behavior* (Stanford, Calif.: Stanford University Press, 1964).

82. J. Garbarino, "The Human Ecology of Child Maltreatment: A Conceptual Model for Research," *Journal of Marriage and the Family* 39 (1977):721-736.

83. Bronfenbrenner, "The Origins of Alienation."

84. E. Wynne, *Growing Up Suburban* (Austin, Texas: University of Texas Press, 1977).

85. J. Garbarino, "The Issue is Human Quality: In Praise of Children," *Children and Youth Services Review* 1 (1979):353-377.

86. J. Garbarino, "The Family: A School for Living," *National Elementary School Principal* 55 (1976):66-70.

2 The Meaning of School Success

An Ecological Perspective on Schooling

What does it mean to succeed in school? To answer this question we must go beyond the confines of the classroom both in time and in space. It is tempting (and educational research has often been tempted) to use academic performance as the operational definition of school success. Most analyses use some combination of standardized tests and grades to measure both success *in* schools and the success *of* schools. Such a definition is inappropriate, however, because it masks many of the key elements of a socially valid analysis, an analysis that can adequately inform public policy. Before we can rationally define school success, we must understand that the meaning of schooling should be linked to the socialization functions it performs. As Inkeles has so aptly stated:

> Socialization research generally begins from the wrong end. . . . The starting point of every socialization study should be a set of qualities "required" by, *i.e.*, maximally adaptive in, a given socio-cultural system and/or manifested in a given population.[1]

The question then becomes how some develop these qualities and why some fail to develop them.

If our concern is human quality, then we are interested in schools and schooling as components of human development and of the socialization process. As discussed in chapter 1, much conventional educational research seeks to describe the "inside" of education; studying education is not really a step toward a larger analytic arena. We must enter that larger analytic arena, however. At stake are our criteria for observing, analyzing, and evaluating education. If we wish to know about the role of school and schooling in development, with the goals of development defined by the roles and characteristics of adulthood, then we need to know where schools and schooling fit into the larger social ecology of human development.

To study the ecology of child development is to undertake the scientific study of how the child develops interactively with the immediate social and physical environment, and how aspects of the larger social context affect what goes on in the child's immediate settings.[2] Within this framework the child is a developing person who plays an active role in an everwidening world. The newborn child shapes the feeding behavior of its mother but is confined largely to a crib or a lap and has only limited means of communicating its needs and wants. The 10-year-old, on the other hand, influences many adults and other children located in many different settings, and has many ways of communicating. The world of adolescents is still larger and more diverse, as is their ability to influence it. Over time, the child and the environment negotiate their relationship through a process of reciprocity. Neither is constant; each depends on the other. One cannot predict the future of either without knowing something about the other. Does a handicapped child stand a greater risk of being abused? It depends. Some environments are more vulnerable than others to the stresses of caring for such a child.[3] Does economic deprivation harm development? Again, it depends on how old one is when deprivation strikes, on one's sex, on what the future brings in the way of vocational opportunity, on the quality of family life in the past, on one's economic expectations and assumptions, and on whether one looks at the short term or at the long run.[4] In short—it depends.

Bronfenbrenner's ecological framework is useful here in that, in addition to recognizing the transactive nature of development, he also considers the multiple levels at which environmental influences originate. Bronfenbrenner has described the individual's environment as "a set of nested structures, each inside the next, like a set of Russian dolls."[5] As we ask and answer questions about development at one level, this ecological framework reminds us to look at the next levels both within and beyond the immediate setting to find the questions to ask and answer. For example, to understand the conflicts of husbands and wives over lost income, we must look outward to the economy that puts the husbands out of work and welcomes the wives in to the labor force, and to the culture that defines a person's personal worth in monetary terms and blames the victims of economic dislocation for their own losses. We must also look inward, to the parent-child relationships that are affected by the changing roles and status of the parents and to the temperamental characteristics of the individuals involved.[6] Further, we must look "across" to see how the several systems involved (family, workplace, and economy) adjust to new conditions over time. These interlocking social systems are the stuff of which ecological analyses are made.

Bronfenbrenner's framework posits four general types of environmental systems, categorized by their proximity to children and by the immediacy of their effects on development. Most immediate to the developing child are *microsystems*. These are the joint product of physical settings and behavioral interactions in which individuals experience and create day-to-day reality. For children, microsystems are the places they inhabit, the people who are there with them, and the things they do together. At first, most children experience only one, quite small microsystem—the home—involving interaction with one person at a time in relatively simple activities such as feeding, bathing, and cuddling. As the child develops, complexity normally increases; the child does more, with more people, in more places.

We know that the management of survival needs (eating, eliminating, and so forth) is a critical task for the developing child's microsystem. Play also figures prominently in the process of the microsystem from the early months of life, eventually being joined by work. Playing, working, and loving—what Freud called the essence of normal human existence—are the principal classes of activities that characterize the child's microsystem. However, the extent to which these activities take place, their quality, and their level of complexity are all variables. An environmental microsystem presents a developmental risk to the child if it is characterized by a narrowly restricted range and level of activities; impoverished experience in playing, working, and loving; or stunted reciprocity where genuine *inter*action is lacking and where either party seeks to avoid or be impervious to the other. Such neglect and rejection are developmentally dangerous.[7] At the microsystem level, environmental opportunities for a child are provided by enduring, reciprocal, multifaceted relationships that emphasize meeting survival needs, playing, working, and loving.

Mesosystems are the relationships between the contexts, or micro-systems, in which the developing person experiences reality. Important mesosystems for children include relationships between home and school, home and neighborhood, and school and neighborhood. The richness of mesosystems for the child is measured by the number of links, by value consensus, and by the diversity of the microsystems.

The school-home mesosystem is of great developmental significance for the child. In general, we would expect enhanced development in cases where this mesosystem was characterized by a lot of interaction between parents and school personnel, where more was known to members of both settings, and where home and school communicated frequently.[8] However, we must add the proviso

> that such interconnections not undermine the motivation and capacity of those persons who deal directly with the child to act on his behalf. This qualification gives negative weight to actions by school personnel that degrade parents or to parental demands that undermine the professional morale or effectiveness of the teacher.[9]

Those familiar with contemporary schooling know that both these problems exist, particularly in the urban environment. In our diverse cities the quality of school-home mesosystems is variable. Indigenous paraprofessionals, home visits, and parent-teacher organizations all can contribute to enhancing the positive significance of school-home mesosystems.

The stronger, more positive, and more diverse the links between settings, the more powerful and beneficial the resulting mesosystems will be as an influence on the child's development. A rich range of mesosystems is a developmental opportunity, whereas a poor set of mesosystems produces impaired development—particularly when home and school are involved. The quality of the child's mesosystems often is determined by events in systems where the child herself does not participate but where things happen that have a direct impact on her parents and other adults who do interact with her. Bronfenbrenner calls these settings *exosystems*.

Exosystems are situations that have a bearing on a child's development but in which the developing child herself does not actually play a direct role. The child's exosystems are those settings that have power over her life, although she does not participate in them. They include the workplaces of parents (with which most children do not have direct contact), and those centers of power such as school boards and planning commissions that make decisions affecting the child's day-to-day life. These exosystems enhance development when they make life easier for parents and undermine development when they make life harder for parents. Thus, exosystem opportunity lies in those situations in which there are forces at work outside the family on behalf of children and their parents. When childrearing is supported by those in high places, the opportunities for child development increase. The initiative taken by the politically powerful Kennedy family as advocates in the federal government on behalf of retarded children is an example, although institutions (offices and structures) in the exosystem are generally of greater importance than individuals.[10]

In exosystem terms, environmental risk occurs in two ways. First, institutions may affect parents or other significant adults in a child's life in a way that impoverishes their behavior in the child's microsystem. For example, Kohn found that when parents work in settings that demand conformity rather than self-direction, they reflect this orientation in their childrearing, thereby stifling important aspects of the child's development.[11] Other examples include elements of a parent's working experience that result in an impoverishment of family life, such as long or inflexible hours, extensive traveling, or stress. Second, risk may flow from the exosystem when decisions are made in those settings that adversely affect the child or treat her unfairly. For example, when the school board suspends extracurricular programs in the child's school, or when the planning commission runs a highway through the child's neighborhood, they jeopardize the child's development. Thus, exosystem risk comes when the child lacks effective advocates in decision-making bodies. Albee has gone as far as to identify powerlessness as the primary factor leading to impaired development and psychopathology.[12] It certainly plays a large role in determining the fate of groups of children, and it may even be very important in individual cases—such as whether or not a youth's parents have enough influence to get her a second chance when she gets into trouble at school or with the police. At the exosystem level, risk is often a political matter.

Meso- and exosystems are embedded in the broad ideological and institutional patterns of a particular culture or subculture—how the ecological pieces fit together. These patterns are the *macrosystem*—the "blueprints" for that culture's ecology of human development. These blueprints reflect a people's shared assumptions about how things should be done. A macrosystem is the set of norms about how development proceeds and the appropriate nature and structure of micro-, meso-, and exosystems. Conventional cultural and ethnic labels (such as Latin, Italian, or Indian) suggest unique clusters of ideological and behavioral patterns. Beyond these labels, however, these ideologies and behaviors need to be operationalized and their implications for child development examined. We need to know, for example, how similar (in terms of their consequences for parents and children) are the processes of responding to economic crisis in two different cultures? How does the school-home mesosystem work in two different ethnic groups? Having different labels does not mean that we necessarily have different macrosystems. For example, the definition of child abuse varies relatively little among ethnic groups in the United States.[13]

In macrosystem terms, environmental opportunity is a prochild ideology. For example, a society's assumption that families stricken by economic or medical tragedy have a right to public support represents macrosystem opportunity, as does strong political base of support for child services.

What constitutes environmental risk with respect to macrosystems? It is an ideology or cultural alignment that threatens to impoverish children's microsystems and mesosystems, and that sets exosystems against them. It can be a national economic policy that tolerates or even increases the chances of economic dislocations and poverty for families with young children. It can be institutionalized support for high levels of geographic mobility that disrupts neighborhood and school connections and the social networks of parents. It can be a pattern of nonsupport for parents that tolerates or even aggravates intense conflicts between the roles of worker and parent. It can be patterns of racist, sexist, or other values that demean large numbers of parents, thereby undermining the psychological security of their children and threatening each child's self-esteem. In general, macrosystem risk is any social pattern or societal event that impoverishes the ability and willingness of adults to care for children and of children to learn from adults.

In summary, environmental influences on the child's development originate from systems at all four levels in the human ecology of the child. Because systems at each level have distinctive characteristics that are relevant to a child's development, different criteria are appropriate for assessing the impacts of each level on the child. Further, these effects may be either positive or negative—either opportunities or risks. Finally, although the family microsystem is usually the most-important system for a child, the overall impact of the environment emerges from the dynamic balance among all influences over time.

The importance of the various environmental systems and the interactions among them are described well by deLone.[14] He notes that young children rarely experience social class directly but that school, neighborhood, and family filter these influences.

> The nature of a society at a given time shapes the structure of social classes; social class influences the nature of family life and experience; racial membership influences likely occupation; through income, occupation helps determine neighborhood. In the midst of this complex, breathing organism called social structure is the child.[15]

The issues facing educators are enduring ones. When our social life was simple and traditional moral agencies were effective, the school could be a place where children were trained to acquire and use the linguistic tools needed in the personal acquisition of knowledge. But with home, church, and neighborhood life weakening, the school carries an additional burden, becoming one of the nation's chief moral teachers. Thus, we have come a long way from simple alphabetic instruction.

> There is then the need that the school shall train the total personality of a pupil for the total obligation of social life. . . . The school of the future will perform an educational function as broad as human life itself. . . . It is inevitably destined by force of surrounding circumstances to become the center of community life. . . .[16]

Suzzallo wrote these words in 1911, but the issues for educators are as clear now as they were then, and just as difficult, if not more so. They all revolve around the goals of education and the means for reaching these goals.

The Purposes of Education

At the heart of any discussion of the meaning of school success is a basic issue: What are the purposes of education? This question is at once philosophical, political, ethical, sociological, and anthropological. The literature of educational philosophy abounds with discussions of just this point; what *should* education seek to accomplish? The more empirically oriented inductive social sciences, on the other hand, seek to discover the actual functions of education and how these fit in with the overall institutional ideological structure of the society (the macrosystem). A complete analysis naturally must incorporate elements of both these approaches. Since we began with a concern for the dynamics of human developmental purpose, we are impelled to consider more than simply what *is*. Rather, a concern for habitability (that is, the quality of the social environment) requires that we assess what *is needed* as a basis for deciding what *should be*. Having done this, we can take an informed look at what is. This interplay of possibility, actuality, and developmental necessity is at the heart of an ecological perspective on schools and schooling.

Any ecologically adequate definition of the purposes of education must have a developmental perspective. This becomes crucial in a discussion of schooling in the United States because educational policy as formulated and implemented often lacks a developmental perspective. The European tradition is richer in this respect, as the classic formulation by the sociologist Emile Durkheim demonstrates. He argued that the purpose of education is to arouse and develop in the child a certain number of physical, intellectual, and moral states, which are demanded of him by both the political society as a whole and the special milieu for which he is specifically destined.[17]

Although this definition is a good starting point, it is, as we shall see in the course of our discussion, not fully adequate in all respects. However, it does sensitize us to the broad social role of schooling. The issues here are complex; they are, in fact, particularly complex and difficult in the modern United States. U.S. schools have tended to maintain a dual system. On the one hand, the day-to-day principles of the classroom are quite limited in their focus. The official line, on the other hand, is so broad and all encompassing as to be little more than a vague pro forma statement of the principles of self-actualization and of Western civilization. For example, consider the "goals of education" in New York State.

New York State Goals of Education

1. Mastery of the basic skills of communication and reasoning essential to live a full and productive life.
2. Ability to sustain lifetime learning in order to adapt to the new demands, opportunities, and values of a changing world.
3. Ability to maintain one's mental, physical, and emotional health.
4. Understanding of human relations—respect for and ability to relate to other people in our own and other nations, including those of different sexes, cultures, and aspirations.
5. Competence in the processes of developing values, particularly in the formation of the spiritual, ethical, religious, and moral values that are essential to individual dignity and a humane civilization.

6. Knowledge of the humanities, social sciences, and natural sciences at a level required to participate in an ever more complex world.
7. Occupational competence necessary to secure employment commensurate with ability and aspiration and to perform work in a manner that is gratifying both to the individual and to those served.
8. Knowledge and appreciation of our culture and capacity for creativity, recreation, and self-renewal.
9. Understanding of the processes of effective citizenship in order to participate in and contribute to the government of our society.

In point of fact, the purposes and scope of education in the United States, although seeming reasonably clear to Durkheim and to the New York State Department of Education, are increasingly subject to debate in some fundamental ways. Writing in an important book on the socialization of youth, Burton White stated the problem as follows:

> Modern societies require educational institutions, but then the more important questions still remain: who will participate? what form will educational institutions take? how will they mix with other institutions of society?[18]

It is encouraging that these questions are asked. Out of this search for "new" answers may come a willingness to reformulate some of our "old" notions about schools and schooling. It suggests that the contemporary ideological climate may be responsive to a new approach, in particular to an ecological approach that attempts to define school success with reference to the issues of social and historical context.

We may wish to consider two principal questions about schools and schooling. One deals with the school as a context for human development, with the role of the school in facilitating the growth and development of the individual and, indeed, of the entire society. We can justifiably ask how successful it is in accomplishing this goal. The second question concerns the role of schools in providing credentials, that is, in providing socioeconomic opportunities to individuals and groups. However, any analysis must begin with the meaning and implications of school success, for both the individual and the society.

The Meaning of School Success: Academic Excellence versus Social Status

In attempting to define success in school, we may usefully consider several possibilities. The first, and perhaps the most obvious from an American standpoint, is "academic excellence." By this we mean, of course, the use of relative distinction on measures of a student's mastery of the curriculum (through assessment by teachers and tests) to determine who is a success and who a failure. The conventional U.S. notion (in contrast to the European view embodied in Durkheim's statement) sees the school as a setting primarily dedicated to cognitive development and to the acquisition of knowledge and intellectual skills. This definition clearly implies academic excellence as the operational definition of school success. In such a conception, whatever social goals are recognized clearly play a peripheral role.

The major purpose of the batteries of tests included in the school's program is the measurement of such academic excellence. Other purposes include the diagnosis of failure and the comparative evaluation of the effectiveness of schools and teachers. Both course grades and standardized achievement tests are designed to provide a quantitative expression of academic excellence. However clear and nearly self-evident the legitimacy and validity of such a definition of school success may appear, it is open to challenge on both theoretical and empirical grounds. Certainly some cultures and social systems radically different from our own would have no qualms about challenging academic achievement as the *raison d'être* of schooling, as many a visitor to China or, for that matter, Europe will attest.[19]

In other words, we have grounds for believing that academic excellence is not the most valid or most significant measure of school success. This evidence comes from a variety of sources, including Coleman's study of high-school students and their values, McClelland's review of grades and testing, and Jencks's and Coleman's assessments of the socioeconomic antecedents and consequences of schooling.[20] For one thing, investigators have shown that indexes of academic excellence bear little relation to important aspects of life success outside of the schools. Thus, high grades and achievement scores, although conceptually and empirically related to each other, either do not relate or relate only weakly to indexes of life success, however measured.[21] People with high grades in school are no more successful, in general, than are those with average (but passing) grades. Thus, the system of academic excellence represented by grades and achievement scores is in most respects a closed system. Success within that system does not directly imply success outside it. Furthermore, within the larger social system of the school, particularly the high school, academic excellence is not particularly important. It ordinarily has relatively little value as social currency in the day-to-day human world of the student, whatever the formal institution itself may say through teachers and parents.

High achievement does relatively little to win respect, friendship, prestige, and status for the student in the eyes of his or her peers. What little it does convey is apparently granted only grudgingly.[22] In fact, academic excellence is likely to elicit a negative social response unless it is linked to some other, more negotiable characteristic such as athletic prowess or extracurricular social leadership. It is presumably for this reason, among others, that in Coleman's studies of high-school students (and elsewhere) measures of academic excellence such as grades reveal only a moderate relationship to intellectual *competence* or *ability*, as measured by intelligence tests and other standard instruments for assessing ability.[23]

This weak relationship seems to indicate that grades do not elicit the full efforts of students and/or that grades are dependent on factors other than intelligence-test scores, that is, on "pure" academic ability. The instruments themselves are reasonably reliable. If grades were eliciting a high level of commitment from students, the correlation of intellectual "ability" to academic performance might be expected to account for more than the approximately 33 percent of the variance in grades that they currently appear to determine ($r = .55$ according to Coleman 1961, or $r = .59$ according to Jencks[24]). The current arrangements governing academic excellence seem oddly at variance with the developmental needs and motives of the students. It appears that the interest, time, effort, and resources of students are largely directed elsewhere—a phenomenon of which teachers, parents, and adolescents are clearly aware. "Our data also convey the impression that large numbers of junior and senior high school students are preoccupied with, and favorably impressed by interests and activities other than academic ones."[25] Although it does command the attention of most of the students some of the time, and of some of the students most of the time, academic achievement is not solidly supported by a broad consensus of values and motives. This lack of social relevance in measures of academic excellence presents a second rationale for questioning any definition of school success that relies primarily on grades and/or achievement-test scores.

It seems unwise to establish academic performance as the principal component of school success because it fails to relate adequately to important features of life success outside the immediate school setting. In both the short and the long run, it does not play a vital role in the social system of students and apparently does not elicit student efforts commensurate with their ability. Given the pivotal role of the school in the day-to-day life of the student, any index of success must do more than assess superior functioning within the temporary confines of that system as it exists in the formal, adult-defined grading structure. We therefore wish to discard academic performance per se. In doing so, however, we do not want to downgrade it as a goal. The value of academic excellence as an underpinning of much that is good in our civilization cannot be denied. However, as the prime criterion of school success it leaves much to be desired. What else, then, may be considered in its place?

If anthropology has taught us anything, it has shown us the need to *begin* any study of social behavior with a recognition of and respect for the values and beliefs of the "natives." This assertion of cultural relativism as a basic analytic perspective is useful in the present context. To understand why people succeed in schools, we need to know what they judge success to be. Schools exist through the behavior of the participants as well as in the formal ideology of the institutions and persons to whom they are officially responsible. For our purposes, then, we must examine the meaning of school success in the eyes of the students. If teachers are inclined to define success as academic achievement (their terms), students are more likely to define success in terms of peer social status (their terms). In such a conception, school success is the recognition and respect offered by significant others in the student's life—principally peers. Coleman offers support for such a conception.

> The fundamental competition in a high school is neither for grades, nor for athletic achievement, nor any other such activity. It is a competition for recognition and respect—the elements of which status is composed—in the eyes of one's fellows and the opposite sex.[26]

The possibility of using peer social status as the major criterion for defining social success is alluring because it speaks directly to the need to understand the school setting in the terms of the participants and thus goes far toward meeting the requirements of anthropological validity. Furthermore, it focuses on interaction patterns within the school as a context for human development. Given that students are motivated to attain the recognition and respect of significant others, social status can provide a basis for assessing what the criteria for success are—that is, what it takes to gain recognition and respect—and, in turn, who succeeds. Coleman's analysis does just that, with the conclusion that athletics (for boys) and extracurricular social activities (for girls), much more than academic performance, are the main criteria of school success. The relative importance of academic performance as a component in peer social status has been found to vary (within limits) from school to school, as a function of a variety of contextual and climate factors.[27] Coleman carried out his analyses in the late 1950s and early 1960s, but subsequent researchers have substantially confirmed the original findings.[28]

However, peer social status may not be the best choice as an overall index of school success because it does not relate directly enough to the cognitive goals, purposes, and functions of the school, and it appears to lack an adequate dimension of "durability." It does not do comprehensive justice, any better than does academic achievement, to the broad goals and functions of education described earlier. Although we must begin with cultural relativism in understanding students as "natives," we cannot in good scholarly conscience stop there.

One may well ask (as some have in the popular literature) what has become of the most-popular students of yearbooks gone by.[29] If academic excellence is inappropriate because it tends to ignore social competence—indeed, the entire social system—then social status is likewise incomplete because it focuses too exclusively on nonacademic factors. Both indexes are insufficiently comprehensive to do justice to the broad role of the schools in the human and humane development of the child and adolescent. What we need is some operational compromise that allows for both the social authority of teachers in defining the criteria for school success and the power of the student natives in shaping the meaning of doing well in school.

The Meaning of School Success: Toward an Index with Ecological and Predictive Validity

There is a third possibility, one that appears to fulfill the necessary conditions. This third index is educational attainment, the number of years of schooling completed. Educational attainment means the development of academic skills, social relations, and educational interest sufficient to produce continued participation in formal educational settings. Hence, it appears to be a strong candidate for selection as the most appropriate index of school success. Looked at in the most positive light, it implies an acceptance of the broad goals of schooling. Looked at in the most cynical manner it indicates ability and willingness to "work the system," an aspect of competence that has application to a wide range of situations.

Educational attainment is positively and strongly associated with socioeconomic life success in a way that simple academic excellence is not, and it offers a more realistic and more durable index than does simple peer-group social status. Educational attainment affects the development of attitudes, values, and self-perceptions—characteristics that are in themselves very important. The attainment of adequate educational progress—that is, grades sufficient to ensure promotion and opportunity for further educational participation—is positively related to social status in the school (among most peer groups) and is negatively related to juvenile delinquency and social pathologies of all sorts (in most youth populations). In short, educational attainment is associated with cognitive and social developments leading to life success. Efforts to relate academic excellence—as measured by grades or achievement scores—to later life success have revealed little association between the two.[30] Jencks went further to assess the association between educational attainment and income, and concluded that only a weak relationship was present (although he later acknowledged a stronger relationship).[31] Both correlations account for approximately 11 percent of the variance ($r = .33$). This analysis, however, appears to be the result of an inadequate conception of the meaning of income, one that does not properly consider its role in shaping the human ecological niche in which development occurs.

To treat income as a simple continuum seems ecologically unreasonable. Our concern is with the relationship between income and social habitability, and thus the issue is not simply one of how many dollars one has. Rather, it is a question of having the purchasing power necessary to meet developmental needs. There are a number of ways to represent the difference between income as "raw dollars" and income as defining an ecological niche. In terms of human development, the difference between $5,000 and $10,000 is in no way equivalent to the difference between $30,000 and $60,000 (or $50,000 and $55,000). What matters is the relation of dollar amounts to substantially different patterns of social habitability. We need not rely on purely intuitive speculation in this matter, however. There are data suggesting that educational attainment accounts for more than 80 percent of the *ecologically relevant* variance in income. As Jencks states in a 1979 book updating his earlier work on inequality and education, "The best readily observable predictor of a young man's eventual status or earnings is the amount of schooling he has had."[32] He goes on to note that whereas the first and last years of high school and college appear to be more strongly correlated with increased earnings, the economic benefits of education are not primarily related to certification effects. "Any year of schooling raises earnings to some extent."[33]

The Bureau of Labor Statistics provides sample budgets (for a family of four) to live at several levels of socioeconomic viability. Although these budgets are in some sense arbitrary, they do address the issue of income versus ecological habitability. The other alternatives (for example, using some sort of numerical transformation of raw dollars) may be of use at some point, but for the purposes of this discussion they are perhaps unnecessarily complex and difficult to relate to developmental needs. The bureau's budgets may be used to fix the relation of educational attainment to the probability that human development occurs in different socioeconomic ecologies. This is, of course, the central ecological question. Based on the bureau's budgets, a family of four needs an income of $20,517 to attain what may be termed a comfortable "intermediate-budget" lifestyle (in 1979 dollars).[34] Incomes between $7,942 and $12,585 may be termed struggling ("lower budget"); an income below $7,942 is considered "poverty." These figures, rather than a simple or transformed numerical expression of income, present the most ecologically valid index of socioeconomic success. Naturally, these sample budgets are linked to particular times and places. But that is one of the messages of human ecology: The meaning of any one phenomenon is dependent on its relationship to the context defined by the interdependent social systems surrounding it.

Table 2-1 presents the relationship of educational attainment to presence in different socioeconomic ecologies. It thus allows us to answer the following question: At each level of educational attainment, what percentage of persons are in each socioeconomic ecology?

The racial difference merits comment. Jaffe completed a study of the "gap" based on race.[35] He computed a "dissimilarity index," which reveals the degree to which there is an imbalance between the value of educational attainment in producing access to jobs. He studied the "vocational gap" between whites and blacks at the same level of education. In examining recent trends in this index, he found that the gap was closing and that education was becoming more equally valuable. Racial differences in educational attainment have come to account for more and more of the actual employment gap as vocational barriers based on direct racial discrimination have been reduced.[36]

It seems reasonable to expect this trend to continue and to hope that eventually there will be little or no need for separate columns by race. However, there is still much to be accomplished. As Jencks shows, an extra year of elementary or high school raises whites' occupational status twice as much as that of nonwhites.[37] Interestingly, a B.A. degree is worth more to nonwhites than to whites; but this is probably due more to the relatively low status of nonwhites who do not finish college than to the high status of those who do.[38]

As table 2-1 reveals, there is a very strong relationship between number of years of school completed and the probability that one operates in a socioeconomically favorable environment. This one factor accounts for most of the variance. It seems that it is *through* educational attainment that other factors (socioeconomic background, educational aspirations, academic ability, and so on) have their impact on one's socioeconomic destiny. School success is an important vehicle for access to life success, as defined in socioeconomic and other terms. As others have noted, educational attainment has rapidly become the medium of exchange for "credentializing" and otherwise sorting American youth.[39] It is thus a major vehicle for the haves to hold their ground, as well as the major identifying badge of the have-nots.

The criterion of socioeconomic predictive validity argues powerfully for the importance of educational attainment as an index of school success with significant consequences. The greater the number of years of school successfully completed, the more likely one is to be able to live in socioeconomic comfort or affluence. It is unnecessary, for our purposes, to attempt to establish more than this. Once a level of socioeconomic comfort has been attained—and in many cases even before that level is reached—it

Table 2-1
Percentage in Different Socioeconomic Ecologies, by Educational Attainment

Socioeconomic Ecology

Gross Categories

Educational Attainment	Struggling or Poverty		Comfortable or Affluent	
	Whites (%)	Blacks (%)	Whites (%)	Blacks (%)
1-7 years	82.2	84.0	17.8	10.3
Elementary school				
8 years	75.6	84.3	24.4	15.7
9-11 years	67.6	81.8	32.4	18.2
High school				
12 years	51.8	69.4	48.2	30.6
13-15 years	44.2	65.3	55.8	34.7
College				
16 years	25.7	36.9	74.3	63.4

Detailed Breakdown

Educational Attainment	Poverty		Struggling		Comfortable		Affluent	
	Whites (%)	Blacks (%)	Whites (%)	Blacks (%)	Whites (%)	Blacks (%)	Whites (%)	Blacks (%)
1-7 years	36.3	51.6	45.9	38.1	11.3	5.8	6.5	4.5
Elementary school								
8 years	27.8	41.1	47.8	43.2	13.9	10.5	10.5	5.2
9-11 years	18.3	32.5	49.3	49.3	19.4	11.5	13.0	16.7
High school								
12 years	9.9	26.6	41.9	42.8	24.9	21.2	23.3	9.4
13-15 years	7.2	20.4	37.0	44.9	27.0	18.4	28.8	16.3
College								
16 years	3.3	5.0	22.4	31.9	24.0	27.0	50.3	36.1

seems clear that a different set of motivations may take hold. Thus, given a standard of comfort, it may be dependent on one's personality or "values" whether one devotes oneself to becoming affluent as opposed to seeking other, less-material satisfactions. And it is much more a matter of chance and idiosyncratic traits that determines whether one achieves monetary enrichment once it is sought. It is this phenomenon that is documented in Jencks's findings that the major proportion of variance in income is "unexplained" by conventional background and performance indexes and is attributable to some unmeasured factors such as chance and personality.[40]

One need only examine the personal histories of alumni of major universities to see this phenomenon at work. Whereas some organize their lives around the pursuit of wealth and business success, others may seek out social-service, teaching, or artistic careers. The point, of course, is that in the midst of that diversity, virtually none are poverty stricken and very few struggle (as is documented in table 2-1). This discussion may place in a more reasonable perspective Jencks's often cited conclusion about income: "Neither family background, cognitive skill, education attainment nor occupational status explains much of the variation in men's income."[41] We should note that Jencks's later work acknowledged that background "exerts a larger influence on economic outcomes than past research had suggested, . . . as strong an association as that between education and economic success."[42]

At this point, it is worth reasserting a basic proposition: We must know not simply what the differences are, but what difference the differences make. In terms of human development, only a limited portion of the variance in income merits concern; the rest may be left to economists, political economists, and students of socioeconomic justice. It is one's presence in the different socioeconomic niches, not simply the number of dollars, that best relates to the social quality of life.

Educational attainment has been related to a wide range of important aspects of human development.[43] It is clearly one of the experiences of life that makes a difference. It has manifold significant consequences for social development. Although a detailed examination of these differences and their consequences is beyond the scope of the discussion, at least at this point, a few illustrative examples are in order.

Educational attainment is a powerful predictor of a variety of child-care behaviors. For example, it is associated with a pattern of parent-child interaction that facilitates the development of a cognitively sophisticated use of language.[44] Such use of language itself has been related to later academic development.[45] Thus educational attainment results in the transmission of academic achievement. Schooling facilitates cognitive sophistication both directly and through the kinds of activities it presents. In their review of research on cognitive development in a variety of cultures, Michael Cole and Sylvia Scribner point to the importance of the experience of "Western-type" schooling.[46]

> In activities, language is used out of context for special analytical purposes, and the new tool of written language is made available for cognitive operations. School learning thus demands, and fosters abstract modes of thought.[47]

This effect on thinking apparently generalizes from directly intellectual reasoning to political and moral thinking. In a far-reaching survey of political values, practices, and analysis in five nations (Great Britain, Mexico, West Germany, Italy, and the United States), Almond and Verba found that differences in educational attainment among the countries accounted for most of the differences in political values and behavior observed in the study.[48] The higher the level of educational attainment, the greater the political competence and the smaller the differences among nations. As educational attainment increases, particularism tends to decrease and a more "universal" cultural pattern emerges (at least among these Western nations). This finding generalizes to moral judgment and other cognitively based social behaviors.[49]

> Educational systems vary, yet there is a certain uniformity in the educational experience; thus these people share a common experience. Those with less education share less of a common cross-cultural experience with one another and are more affected by the particular history and culture of their own national systems.[50]

This relative homogeneity of schooling is important. It is worth noting here because it echoes Cole and Scribner's conclusions about cognitive development generally when they speak of a Western-type school. Although differences among schools are clearly apparent, these differences may be of limited importance when compared with those found in situations or experiences from which schools and schooling are absent or are of some *radically different* kind. It appears to be the aggregate impact of the experience of schooling that is of greatest importance. Anderson presents this hypothesis very clearly.[51] He notes that we must be cognizant of the differences between macro and micro effects. If all children in a society are exposed to schooling, the effect may be (and certainly seems to be) enormous, "without any individual receiving a different benefit."[52]

The degree to which educational attainment is a basis for homogenizing a society (through universal participation and uniformity of content) is itself an important dependent variable. The role of schooling in the socioeconomic and political life of the society does vary appreciably from nation to nation. The comparison of even such relatively similar societies as the United States and the United Kingdom reveals significant differences in the role of schools and schooling in the social order, as Turner discovered in his analysis of socioeconomic mobility in the two countries.[53] The relative homogeneity of schooling in the United States may, in fact, be one of the distinguishing characteristics of our society. Judith Torney studied the relative impact of various socializing agents in ten nations and found that, "in comparison to the other countries tested . . . the influence of school factors upon cognitive and attitudinal outcomes was smallest in the United States."[54] This finding parallels analyses of the general impact of schooling on life outcomes.

We must compare human ecologies in which schooling plays substantially different roles if we are to know how to evaluate relatively small differences within ecological settings. This comparative perspective can be invaluable. Where everyone receives schooling that is itself rather homogeneous, there cannot be appreciable differences. This by no means signifies that the experience of schooling is not one of great importance. On the contrary, comparisons of "high-schooling" versus "low-schooling" settings both within and across societies reveal large and important differences. It is the impact of the relatively small but important differences among Western-type schools that is at issue in any society characterized by comprehensive schooling.

Whereas academic excellence apparently does not play the critical role in the social system of the school, "nonfailure" is another matter. To be socially successful (in most peer groups) a modicum of academic competence is certainly valuable. Peck and Gallini found that socially successful high-school students—members of the "leading crowd"—had better than average grades.[55] This parallels Coleman's findings.[56] The degree to which the leading crowd's grades were above average for any particular school was apparently a function of the degree to which academic success was valued in that school. This in turn, for the most part, was itself determined by the background of the student body, that is, the academic orientation of their parents. For the purposes of this discussion, the important point is that academic failure was not ordinarily associated with social success. It seems that minimal academic competence is a kind of necessary condition for social success—the respect and recognition for which individuals strive.

Complementary evidence comes from studies of juvenile delinquency. It appears that academic failure is consistently associated with delinquency. That is, if minimal competence and progress are not attained, the student faces a difficult psychological problem because of the isolation and damaged self-esteem that accompany such failure. The resolution of that problem is likely to be delinquent behavior.[57] Gold has reviewed the evidence on this issue and has concluded that adolescents generally see schooling in terms of preparation for adulthood.[58] Thus, when they fail in school they feel jeopardized. Delinquents resemble nondelinquents in their basic appreciation of the importance of school. He concludes that those who give up on school and are delinquent do so "not because school is irrelevant but too relevant."[59]

Substandard academic performance tends to lead to discrimination in the social system of the school—most clearly in large schools. Barker and Gump reported significant discrimination against academically marginal students (that is, students who experience academic failure and who by virtue of background and performance are most likely to drop out).[60] Such students do not receive opportunities and encouragements by either peers or adults to participate in school activities. Such marginal students reveal a corresponding lack of citizenship and sense of responsibility compared with academically successful students evidencing normal competence. This pattern of discrimination suggests that academic failure tends to disqualify the individual from full studenthood and corresponding peer status.[61]

The use of educational attainment as the index of school success has much to recommend it. It incorporates the development of sufficient academic skills to achieve at a level that allows promotion and future opportunities for participation—most importantly, high-school graduation and access to college. It implies a pattern of motivation and interest that promotes overall personal development. Another factor coincident with academic and social success as a function of educational attainment is socioeconomic placement. Whereas academic excellence does not weigh heavily in favor of the student's present and future socioeconomic success and personal development, academic failure tends to disqualify and alienate him, thereby disrupting his present as well as undermining his future. It appears theoretically and empirically reasonable to use educational attainment—satisfactory progress rather than relative academic excellence or peer social status—as the focus of our analysis of schooling in the United States, its successes and failures, both individual and social.

The Implications of School Success for Social and Individual Development

What can we say about the social history of school success in America? During the second half of the nineteenth century there were regional differences in the enrollment of school-age children and adolescents.[62] According to recent U.S. Bureau of the Census reports, these regional problems persist, although they have diminished somewhat over time.

As we have noted before, the *meaning* of school attendance has changed. In 1870 the average student had a 132-day school term but was out of school some 41 percent of the time. By 1920 the average term was 162 days, and the average student was out 25 percent of the time, By 1968 the term was 179 days, and the student was out only 9 percent of the time.[63]

However, as Clark has noted:

> The national averages obscure great differences among types of schools in attendance rates. In some inner-city schools currently, a quarter or a third, or more of the students may be missing on a given day.[64]

The point is that absence, which today indicates deviance, was in fact normal in earlier times. The difference in attendance rates of some inner city schools and in the behavior of their students is an important one. Likewise, regional differences in enrollment portend important differences in social climate.[65] These differences have an impact on all the life outcomes linked to school success.

A final historical illustration is found in the fact that, whereas in 1937 only 42 percent of those who were enrolled in the fifth grade actually completed high school and only 15 percent entered college, by 1977 these figures were 85 percent and 49 percent, respectively.[66]

These data indicate a pattern of ever increasing school success. More and more people are finishing high school and enrolling in institutions of higher education. The most-recent data indicate a leveling off of this upward trend. Presumably the number of people attaining a basic level of mastery in academic skills—reading and arithmetic—has risen in a parallel fashion, although recent estimates indicate that one in five U.S. residents is functionally illiterate (that is, unable to understand everyday written materials such as newspapers). The major force propelling this development appears to have been not some new technique of instruction or curriculum innovation but, rather, a series of events set off by the overall socioeconomic development of the society. The diffusion of relative material prosperity in the post-World War II era led to this advance in general school success by realizing the widespread preexisting popular support for schooling as a worthwhile endeavor.[67] It would seem at first glance—particularly given what has gone before—that this historical development should be accepted as an unqualified social and individual good. However, this good may have brought some serious adverse consequences. Ecology always looks for the unintended consequences of events, however benign these may appear at first glance.[68] In other words, what is the cost of the gains in school success reported earlier?

Although we easily see the positive outgrowths of the historical pattern of school success—a more highly skilled labor force and greater political literacy, to cite but two examples—it is harder to see the negative outcomes.[69] An ecological perspective insists on an analysis in terms of the contribution of this phenomenon to the quality of life in the society.

Whereas in 1938 a person who did not complete high school was part of the majority (58 percent of the students who began fifth grade did not graduate from high school), today he is a member of a relatively small minoriy (less than 15 percent). As a minority-group member, he is discriminated against socioeconomically; he is less likely to earn an income in the "comfortable" range and is more likely to be unemployed.[70] He is defined as part of the "dropout problem" and is under some pressure to return to school.[71] Consider, for example, the media campaigns directed at dropouts and employing entertainment and sports stars. The title of a mid-1960s collection of major readings on education *(Profile of the School Drop-Out: A Reader on America's Major Educational Problem)* illustrates this development. What are the human consequences of this state of affairs?[72]

Perhaps high schools and colleges today contain many students who in an earlier time would not be there. Are these students content? A recent detailed survey of high-school students concluded that 50 percent of the students were in some way seriously alienated from school.[73] Are these the same students who would have been able to leave school *honorably* and to *find work* in an earlier age, but who are now pressured to remain in school by counselors, the job market, and their own understanding of the world?

There is evidence that one consequence of the increase in school success has been a kind of "credentials inflation"—that is, the same job now requires more schooling than it did a generation ago, so that dropouts find themselves in competition for jobs with those who have a high-school diploma.[74] At the same time, many jobs that at one time required only high-school graduation now set a college degree as a minimum criterion for employment. Furthermore, research surveys indicate that job satisfaction is judged *within* occupational groupings, and not directly as the result of comparisons across groups. Thus, satisfaction is not a function either of educational attainment or of socioeconomic status.[75] Approximately the same proportion are satisfied with their work at each level of the occupational hierarchy. As Campbell has noted, human beings are able to adjust their criteria of need to meet virtually any increase in their standard of living.[76] Clearly, then, although there have been gains from this history of increased school success, these gains have not come without costs. Such is the process of change in the human ecology, particularly change as fundamental as a massive increase in school success.

Why do students attend college? Many apparently do so with little explicit purpose, simply because it is part of the expectations of what is normal that they share with parents, peers, and counselors. Are the nation's colleges becoming full of students who are enrolled not because of some intrinsic interest in education or some sense of cultural and social-class loyalty, but only to escape the economic blackmail and social blackball imposed on them for nonattendance? Does the expectation of socioeconomic discrimination provide the motivation for attendance? There is evidence that the conflict between economic and intellectual orientations toward college provides much of the fuel for campus unrest.[77] Nations that overproduce and underemploy college graduates (such as India and some of the other developing nations) find themselves faced with a malcontented and alienated group whose resentment is potentially (and often actually) socially disruptive.[78]

These questions, which are both intrinsically interesting and important, have been dealt with inadequately in educational research to date. They represent a different type of issue, asking us to measure the value of education and economic opportunity against the effects of alienation and social disruption—the perennial debate between freedom and order. Does our society need so much college? Should we permit such a credentials inflation? Are we really affluent enough to afford all this? In the retrenchment economy of the 1980s, these are difficult but necessary questions. During the 1950s and 1960s colleges grew enormously, with consequences that have not yet been fully comprehended. There is, however, a growing awareness that unlimited growth is potentially dangerous and that "small is beautiful."[79]

Consider the fact that in the United States in the 1970s approximatly 85 percent of the students were completing secondary school and some 43 percent of those students were going on to college, whereas in Great Britain the figures are only 25 percent for completion of secondary school and 6 to 7 percent for college enrollment.[80] Is the habitability of U.S. society proportionally greater than that of British society? Is it fully three times as great, as the relative differences would lead one to expect? Comparisons such as these can be illuminating. Indeed, contrasting the United States and Great Britain is particularly fruitful because the social similarities between the societies highlight differences in the social ecology of education.

One may be tempted to criticize this analysis of school success on the grounds that it is too context bound, too much linked to a particular time and place—to a particular historical setting, institutional configuration, and ideological system. But one of the essential principles of human ecology as a scientific perspective is that the meaning of a phenomenon is to be found in ecological context, triangulated, as it were, by ideology, institutions, and organism. School success is no exception. Its meaning and implications can change as its role in the human ecology changes. As the role of school success in the United States has grown, it may have set in motion a series of readjustments in the operation, structure, and function of schools and other systems. We may be only just beginning to see the consequences of these changes in the systems themselves (for example, within the schools) and in the relations among systems (for example, in the relationship of schooling to vocational success and socioeconomic placement).

The ecological perspective posits social habitability as the ethical prime directive.[81] What is the gain if academic progress generates alienation? Given the relationship of gains in school success to trends in social history, are we not experiencing a conflict between the development of competence and the development of identity? The overriding theme of the second and third quarters of the twentieth century seems to be increases in technological and material competence at the expense of social identity. However reactionary the question may appear, it seems necessary to ask seriously whether the social history of school success bodes well or ill for U.S. society in both the short and the long run. Will the net result of this development be enhanced human development? Will it result in enhanced social habitability of the human environment, as school success has done for specific individuals? Will it result in greater personal fulfillment and material well-being? Or will we experience a kind of social and economic double-cross in which the overall gains in school success will be offset by alienation in the schools? Will we continue to experience a general credentials inflation throughout the society, with the result being social disruption and a decline in the habitability of the human ecology of the United States? We shall see.

Notes

1. A. Inkeles, "Social Structure and the Socialization of Competence," *Harvard Educational Review* 36 (1966):282.

2. J. Garbarino and M. Plantz, *Urban Environments and Urban Children* (New York: Institute for Urban Education, 1981).

3. M. Young and C. Kopp, "Handicapped Children and Their Families: Research Directions" (Unpublished paper, University of California at Los Angeles, 1980).

4. G. Elder, *Children of the Great Depression* (Chicago: University of Chicago Press, 1974); G. Elder and R. Rockwell, *The Life Course and Human Development: An Ecological Perspective* (Unpublished paper, Boys Town Center for the Study of Human Development, Boys Town, Neb., 1977).

5. U. Bronfenbrenner, *The Ecology of Human Development: Experiments by Nature and Design* (Cambridge, Mass.: Harvard University Press, 1979).

6. Elder, *Children of the Great Depression.*

7. N. Polansky, "An Analysis of Research on Child Neglect: The Social Work Viewpoint," in *Four Perspectives on the Status of Child Abuse and Neglect Research,* ed. Herner et al. (Washington, D.C.: National Center on Child Abuse and Neglect, 1976); R. Rohner, "Love Me, Love Me Not," Human Relations Area Files, New Haven, Conn., 1975.

8. U. Bronfenbrenner, *The Ecology of Human Development.*

9. Ibid., p. 218.

10. Urban planning boards are a good example. See W. Michelson and E. Roberts, "Children and the Urban Environment," in *The Child and the City,* ed. W. Michelson, S. Levine, and A. Spina (Toronto: University of Toronto Press, 1979); D. Barker, comments on "The Spatial World of the Child," in *The Child in the City,* ed. Michelson, Levine, and Spina.

11. M. Kohn, *Class and Conformity: A Study in Values,* 2d ed. (Chicago: University of Chicago Press, 1977).

12. G. Albee, *Politics, Power, Prevention and Social Change* (Paper presented at the Vermont Conference on the Primary Prevention of Psychopathology, Burlington, June 1979).

13. J. Giovanonni and R. Becerra, *Defining Child Abuse* (New York: Free Press, 1979).

14. R. deLone, *Small Futures* (New York: Harcourt, Brace, Jovanovich, 1979).

15. Ibid., pp. 158-159.

16. H. Suzzallo, "The School of Tomorrow," in *The Child in the City,* ed. S. Breckinridge (New York: Arrow Press, 1970, reprint ed.).

17. Durkheim, *Education and Sociology* (New York: Free Press, 1956).

18. B. White, "Current Educational Institutions," *Youth: Transition to Adulthood,* ed. J. Coleman (Chicago: University of Chicago Press, 1974).

19. W. Kessen, ed., *Childhood in China* (New Haven, Conn.: Yale University Press, 1975); Durkheim, *Education and Sociology.*

20. J. Coleman, *The Adolescent Society: The Social Life of the Teenager and Its Impact on Education* (Glencoe, Ill.: Free Press of Glencoe, 1961); D. McClelland, "Testing for Competence Rather Than for Intelligence," *American Psychologist* 28 (1973):1-14; C. Jencks, *Inequality: A Reassessment of the Effect of Family and Schooling in America* (New York: Basic Books, 1972); J. Coleman et al., *Equality of Educational Opportunity* (Washington, D.C.: U.S. Government Printing Office, 1966).

21. McClelland, "Testing for Competence;" Jencks, *Inequality.*

22. Coleman, *The Adolescent Society.*

23. Ibid.

24. Jencks, *Inequality.*

25. J. Goodlad, "How Fares the Common School," *Today's Education* 69 (1980):37-40.

26. Coleman, *The Adolescent Society,* p. 143.

27. S. Boocock, "Toward a Sociology of Learning: A Selected Review of Existing Research," *Sociology of Education* 39 (1966):1-45.

28. S. Eitzen, "Athletics in the Status System of Male Adolescents: A Replication of Coleman's 'The Adolescent Society'," *Adolescence* 10 (1975):267-276.

29. M. Medved and D. Wallechinsky, *What Really Happened to the Class of '65* (New York: Random House, 1976).

30. Jencks, *Inequality.*

31. C. Jencks et al., *Who Gets Ahead?* (New York: Basic Books, 1979).

32. Ibid.

33. Ibid., p. 228.

34. U.S. Department of Labor Bureau of Labor Statistics, "Family Budgets," *Monthly Labor Review* 103 (1980):29.

35. A. Jaffee, W. Adams, and S. Meyers, *Negro Higher Education in the 1960s* (New York: Praeger, 1968).

36. Ibid.

37. Jencks, *Who Gets Ahead?*

38. Ibid.

39. H. Borow, "Development of Occupational Motives and Roles," in *Review of Child Development Research,* vol. II, ed. L. Hoffman and M. Hoffman (New York: Russell Sage Foundation, 1966).

40. Jencks, *Inequality.*

41. Ibid., p. 226.

42. Jencks, *Who Gets Ahead?,* p. 230.

43. L. Broom and P. Selznick, *Sociology* (New York: Harper and Row, 1968).

44. H. Bee et al., "Social Class Differences in Maternal Teaching Strategies and Speech Patterns," *Developmental Psychology* 1 (1969): 726-734.

45. E. Schaefer, "Parents as Educators: Evidence From Cross-Sectional, Longitudinal and Intervention Research," in *The Young Child,* vol. II, ed. W. Hartup (Washington, D.C.: National Association for the Education of Young Children, 1972).

46. M. Cole and S. Scribner, *Culture and Thought: A Psychological Introduction* (New York: John Wiley and Sons, 1974).

47. Ibid., p. 24.

48. G. Almond and S. Verba, *The Civic Culture: Political Attitudes and Democracy in Five Nations* (Princeton, N.J.: Princeton University Press, 1965).

49. J. Garbarino and U. Bronfenbrenner, "The Socialization of Moral Judgment and Behavior in Cross Cultural Perspective," in *Moral Development and Behavior*, ed. T. Lickona (New York: Holt, Rinehart and Winston, 1976).

50. Almond and Verba, *The Civic Culture,* p. 319-320.

51. A. Anderson, "A Skeptical Note on Education and Mobility," in *Education, Economy and Society: A Reader in the Sociology of Education,* ed. A. Halsey, J. Floyd, and C. Anderson (New York: Free Press, 1961).

52. Ibid., p. 164.

53. R. Turner, "Modes of Social Accent Through Education: Sponsored and Contest Mobility," in *Education, Economy and Society,* ed. Halsey, Floyd, and Anderson.

54. J. Torney, "History of Political Socialization and Review of Research Freuds" (Summary of Remarks for a Symposium on Political Socialization presented at American Psychological Association, Chicago, 30 August 1975).

55. R. Peck and C. Gallini, "Intelligence, Ethnicity and Social Roles in Adolescent Society," *Sociometry* 25 (1962):64-72.

56. Coleman, *The Adolescent Society.*

57. J. Garbarino, "Alienation and Educational Institutions," Final Report to the New York State Assembly Scientific Advisory Committee, Albany, 1973.

58. M. Gold, "Juvenile Delinquency as a Symptom and Alienation," *Journal of Social Issues* 25 (1969):121-135.

59. Ibid., pp. 132-133.

60. R. Barker and P. Gump, *Big School, Small School: High School Size and Student Behavior* (Stanford, Calif.: Stanford University Press, 1964).

61. E. Keislar, "Experimental Development of 'Like' and 'Dislike' of Others Among Adolescent Girls," *Child Development* 32 (1961):59-66.

62. J. Folger and C. Nam, *Education of the American Population* (Washington, D.C.: U.S. Government Printing Office, 1967).

63. J. Coleman, *Youth: Transition to Adulthood,* Report of the Panel on Youth of the President's Science Advisory Committee (Washington, D.C.: U.S. Government Printing Office, 1973).

64. K. Clark, "Education in the Ghetto: A Human Concern," *Urban Education in the 70s: Reflections and a Look Ahead,* ed. A. Passow (New York: Columbia University, Teachers College Press, 1971), p. 100.

65. J. Garbarino, "Some Thoughts on School Size and Its Effects on Adolescent Development," *Journal of Youth and Adolescence* 9 (1980): 19-31.

66. U.S. Bureau of the Census, U.S. Department of Commerce, "Student Enrollment—Social and Economic Characteristics of Students: October, 1974," *Current Population Reports* no. 278 (1975).

67. Borow, "Development of Occupational Motives."

68. B. Commoner, *The Closing Circle: Nature, Man and Technology* (New York: Alfred A. Knopf, 1971); E. Willems, "Relations of Models to Methods in Behavioral Ecology" (Paper presented at the Biennial Conference, International Society for the Study of Behavioral Development, Guildford, Surrey, England, 13-19 July 1975).

69. Borow, "Development of Occupational Motives"; Almond and Verba, *The Civic Culture.*

70. Borow, "Development of Occupational Motives."

71. E. Douvan and M. Gold, "Modal Patterns in American Adolescence," in *Review of Child Development Research,* vol. II, ed. Hoffman and Hoffman.

72. D. Schreiber, *Profile of the School Dropout: A Reader on America's Major Educational Problem* (New York: Random House, 1967).

73. New York State Commission to Study the Causes of Campus Unrest, "Academy or Battleground: Third Report" (Albany, 1972).

74. R. Boudon, *Education, Opportunity and Social Inequality: Changing Prospects in Western Society* (New York: John Wiley and Sons, 1974).

75. Jencks, *Inequality.*

76. A. Campbell, "Subjective Measures of Well Being," *American Psychologist* 31 (1976):117-124.

77. D. Yankelovich Inc., *The Changing Values on Campus: Political and Personal Attitudes of Today's College Students* (New York: Washington Square Press, 1972).

78. N. Jayaram, "Sadhus No Longer: Recent Trends in Indian Student Activism," *Higher Education* 8 (1979):695-698.

79. E. Schumacher, *Small is Beautiful: Economics as if People Mattered* (New York: Harper and Row, 1973).

80. Silberman, *Crisis in the Classroom.*

81. Willems, "Relations of Models in Ecology."

3 The Origins of School Success

Who Succeeds and Why

Who succeeds in school? Why do some succeed while others fail? These are important questions. How we answer them tells us much both about our own social philosophy and the nature of our society. If we are to understand the school as a context for human development, we must know who succeeds and why others fail. Our society's philosophical and constitutional commitments to justice and equality demand answers.

Two extreme perspectives shape the rhetoric of our answers to the question of school success. Both reflect political conceptions of schooling and its relation to the larger social order. One reflects a conservative/ meritocratic view and the other a progressive/egalitarian outlook.[1] In answer to the questions of who succeeds and why, the conservative/ meritocratist argues: "The talented and righteous succeed in school. They do so because they are intelligent and industrious, whereas the failures are dull and slothful." According to this view, it is solely the quality of the *students* (intellectually, motivationally, and morally) that accounts for observed differences in success.

In contrast, the progressive/egalitarian sees the origins of school success in the class- and culture-bound expectations of the people who run the major institutions of the society—educational, industrial, and political. "The economically privileged and socially sophisticated succeed in school. They do so because they bring with them a stamp of approval and a set of intellectual and emotional habits. These habits correspond to the expectations of teachers, whereas the failures do not know how to play by the 'rules of the game,' rules that exist on behalf of those who already possess socioeconomic and political resources."

These two contrasting positions highlight issues of equality of opportunity. If we accept the conservative/meritocratic view, then the fault lies with the "victims" of failure themselves. The schools are thus blameless. If we apply the progressive/egalitarian approach, then the schools are part of a general conspiracy on behalf of the dominant groups in the society; equality of opportunity is but a rationalizing delusion. The debate implicit in the conflict between the "right" and the "left" on this matter finds expression in a host of related issues, including the role of genetic factors in intellectual development and other aspects of the nature-nurture controversy.[2] The continuing debate over the reliability and validity of testing is another broad issue that derives much of its dynamics from the conflict between the conservative/meritocratic and progressive/egalitarian views.[3] Affirmative action is another such issue.[4]

The conservative/meritocratic view has predominated in the United States throughout most of our history, from the earliest commentators to contemporary teachers. This view is consonant with the individualist ideology that prevades all facets of our institutional life.[5] We see failure as the product of some internal defect. Much as one might like to think otherwise, educational institutions in the United States have traditionally supported this view, as Greer has demonstrated in "The Great School Legend."[6] The only thread of collectivism running through the history of the school's allegiance to the conservative/meritocratic position has been the willingness to see talent and righteousness as the common character of some ethnic and racial groups, whereas dullness and sloth have been attributed to others. Even this has allowed for the "exception that proves the rule," for individuals who do not conform to the supposed natural pattern of their group.

Greer's historical account reveals that on the whole U.S. schools have traditionally sided with the conservative/meritocratic explanation of success and failure. It is, of course, the most effective way to explain away the failure of large groups of children, those who are somehow "alien" to the ethos of the U.S. classroom. In an essay about the "images of schools" in the United States, Margaret Mead pointed out that although the specific terminology used to "explain" the failure of "aliens" may change, the basic rejection of such foreigners continues.

> But the terms "lack of manners," "lack of respect," and "unwillingness to work," which reflect the more moralistic tone of the past, or the words "disturbed children," which reflect the psychiatrically oriented thinking of the present, refer substantially to the same condition.[7]

The current crop of aliens varies somewhat from region to region, but basically includes poor blacks, those with Spanish surnames, American Indians, and some poor whites. When they go to school, these children truly are strangers in a strange land.

Is this rejection inevitable? Certainly some individual teachers and even entire schools are not infected—from a cross-cultural perspective, even entire social systems. We can usefully consider the reports from observers of education in the People's Republic of China, a society radically committed to the progressive/egalitarian position in its most extreme form. In describing Chinese schools, a U.S. delegation reported that the Chinese belief in equality led to a belief in each child; to be sure, there were some children who were slow, but they were never abandoned; the teachers never gave up.[8] Is our commitment to the potential of all children as great as that of the Chinese? The answer is a disappointing "no."

During the era of President Kennedy's New Frontier (1960-1962) and of President Johnson's Great Society (1962-1968) an upsurge of progressive ideology born of affluence infused the institutional life of the United States. For schools this meant widespread adoption, at least publicly, of the progressive/egalitarian view of school success. Some developmental psychologists fueled this change with their promises that a strong and early "dose" of language skills and cognitive stimulation would erase the educational deficits that prevent large numbers of children from succeeding in school.[9] Hunt's 1961 book, *Intelligence and Experience*, was a prime example.[10] According to the popular understanding of Hunt's thesis, early intervention could "inoculate" children against school failure. The assumption underlying these efforts was that one could make all children come to school "talented and righteous" through an intensive cram course during the year preceding the start of school that would give such children a "head start."

Although there is much disagreement regarding the long-term effectiveness of such programs, it does seem clear that they fell far short of the goals of eradicating failure and ensuring equality of opportunity.[11] A report issued by the Stanford Research Institute (prepared for DHEW) reviewed the findings of a number of studies of program evaluation and found that they "uniformly indicate" that

> no known, broadly implemented, treatment or pre-school experience can ensure children from low-income families against later school failure or have a lasting effect on the cognitive abilities or skills of these children independent of later intervention.[12]

These findings conform to the anecdotal accounts of individual superteachers who have achieved success in their classrooms in stimulating talent and motivation among students already defined as failures, only to see it dissipated when the students move on to the less rarefied atmosphere of classrooms run by less-than-extraordinary persons. This is the sad tale recounted by Kohl in *36 Children* and by others who ventured into the classroom as superteachers during the progressive mid-1960s.[13] Although we certainly acknowledge that some dedicated individuals will make a difference in the lives of some children (and we applaud their efforts), "common sense suggests that such interventions are likely to be the exception, not the rule."[14] We are not going to change society in any demonstrable way through programs that deal only with the individual, ignoring the context in which she or he lives. We simply have neither the social technology nor the educational expertise to do so.

It seems that one cannot inoculate children against school failure if the odds are against them. But what are those odds, and what are their origins? This returns us to the initial twofold question: Who succeeds in school, and why do they succeed while others fail? We must consider these questions in what might be called a radical manner. That is, we need to go to the roots of the phenomena, to return to the fundamental events and experiences of schooling. This radical analysis asks us to put aside, at least temporarily, what we think we "know" to be the answers. It asks us to start with the most basic events of schooling and to build our final explanation from there. Research on academic achievement (as distinguished from school success as we are using the concept) has resulted in some very complex and technically sophisticated analyses. Some of the most powerful statistical procedures have been brought to bear on this topic, but few of these studies have attempted a radical look at school success.[15]

The key to an appropriate analysis of the origins of school success is to insist on a simultaneous assessment of each system in the enduring social reality of the student (organism, immediate setting, institutions, and ideology). This is essential because the importance of any particular arrangement of one system is a function of the status of all the others. In a sense, these organism—environment adjustments *are* social reality. We can assess the importance of each element only in terms of its contribution to the total context. It is hoped that this elusive idea will become clearer as we proceed to outline some working hypotheses and examine the data that address them. In doing this, we examine the basic conditions underlying school success. It is a process in which the dividing line between the profound and the simplistic is often unclear.

The First Condition: Support for Attendance

First, the child must be allowed to attend school. Obviously, if children are either formally or informally excluded from school, they cannot, by definition, succeed in school. Although this idea is in many ways too simple to have figured in most analyses of success in the classroom, it is quite powerful in its ramifications.

How serious is this problem in modern United States? Although most people seem to take it for granted that this precondition has been met, the evidence argues otherwise. The Children's Defense Fund (CDF), a nonprofit group committed to identifying and meeting the unmet needs of children through legal action and public-policy intervention, produced some of this evidence in their 1974 report, *Children Out of School in America*.[16] The results present a distressing pattern of unmet developmental needs and socially uninhabitable environments that allow those needs to go unmet.

According to data presented in the 1970 U.S. census, nearly 2 million 7-to 17-year-olds (4.2 percent of the total) were out of school in the three months prior to enumeration. This figure included more than 1 million 7- to 15-year-olds (2.9 percent). Fully 800,000 16- to 17-year-olds (10.3 percent) were not attending school during that period. These figures are bad enough, but the picture is really even worse. First, the census figures are very conservative estimates. CDF has identified a number of sources of undernumeration of the census reports. These include the fact that minority children, who are particularly likely to be out of school, are underrepresented in the census; that census procedures tend to miss children from very large families (more than seven persons), who tend to be out of school; and that the structure of the census questionnaire includes children who are considered to be attending school despite spotty attendance. Second, the rates of nonattendance are not distributed uniformly across regions and social classes. For example, the census reports the rate for Mississippi to be 7.8 percent; at the other extreme, the rate for Minnesota is 2.4 percent. A CDF study of selected areas further illuminated this phenomenon.

> In the 30 areas we surveyed we found 5.4 percent of all children 6 to 17 years old out of school for at least 45 days, one quarter of the school year. 19.6 percent of the 16 and 17 year olds we found were out of school.[17]

CDF expressed shock and outrage at this finding. This strong reaction arises from CDF's awareness of the importance of schooling in the lives of children and adolescents. "It rests on the more fundamental and indisputable premise that total denial of schooling is an almost certain guarantee of failure in American society."[18] And it derives from the injustice with which being out of school is concentrated among the groups least able to afford it. "Double Deprivation: The Less They Have the Less They Learn" was the title of an early important article assessing the impact of educational-intervention projects.[19]

The CDF data indicate that the parent's educational background is more important than income as an influence on enrollment. For example, economically comfortable families with little education have a higher rate of nonenrollment than do better-educated low-income families (7 percent versus 3.5 percent).[20] This is what one would expect, given the crucial role of values and modeling in shaping school success. As should be clear from previous discussions, this pattern of nonenrollment is a serious problem for the individuals and communities involved.

The data on regional and social-class differences in the rates of nonattendance led CDF to examine the day-to-day sources of nonattendance. In so doing, CDF was seeking a process explanation. Wolf proposed a distinction between "status" variables (such as race, class, and age) and "process" variables (the events or experiences that "cause" behavior and are themselves associated with the status variables).[21] Process variables often translate sociological phenomena into social-psychological factors. A consideration of the origins of nonattendance is useful in moving the discussion from status variables (region, class, race) to process variables (behavior, resources, and values). In a society such as ours that is explicitly committed to universal elementary and secondary education, the CDF's results with respect to the process variables of nonattendance are quite disturbing.

The CDF study found that the major source of nonattendance is *exclusion* by the schools themselves. Exclusion, not choice, was the main reason that children and adolescents were out of school.[22] Such exclusion comes from many sources and operates in many forms. A first cause of exclusion is the inability of the children, adolescents, and families to meet demands made by the schools for fees, meal charges, books, and other supplies. Clearly, school attendance requires a minimal level of family and personal organization and resources. The necessary level of such organization and resources, however, differs as a function of the supportiveness of the schools and communities themselves. Some areas provide more support than others. Some are rather unsupportive and make many non-negotiable demands.

Free public education still exacts real costs, and some families cannot meet these demands. The source of this incompetence usually derives from some sort of social pathology within and around the family—alcoholism, drug addiction, vocational incompetence, poverty, unemployment, or poor health.[23] This "hard core" of disorganized families, who lack the moral, social, or financial resources to prevent exclusion of their children from school, is a problem for which no adequate solution has been found in the United States. By permitting or even encouraging their children to be out of school, these families truly visit the sins of the fathers on the children.

CDF found that a second reason for exclusion was problems presented by the students to the operation or value base of the schools. Even in the early 1970s, the major source of exclusion for adolescent females was pregnancy. Organismic damage in general was a major rationale for exclusion. Many schools refused to accept students with even moderate physical or mental handicaps, despite mounting nationwide support for institutional integration of the handicapped. The schools seemed to engage in a process of labeling and defining which organisms qualified and which did not. This is part of the more general problem of "labeling," the consequences of which have been investigated by Hobbs and his colleagues.[24] Suspension for "problem behavior" was found to be a third source of exclusion.

In all this the schools seem both victims and victimizers. They are victims of their inability to succeed with children and adolescents who in some way differ from their model of what a student may and should be. They are victims of the forces that cause and allow family disorganization and social pathology to exist. They are victimizers in their narrow understanding of their role in providing a context for human development.

Attendance is the first condition for school success. The CDF report provides an excellent introduction to the analysis of the origins of school success because it points directly to the critical role played by the "habitability" of the social setting of children and adolescents. It highlights the impact on schooling of stress versus support, of demands versus resources, in the lives of families.

The Second Condition: Orientation to Academic Information

The child must attend to and process academic information. To learn what is necessary for advancement, the child must display an adequate combination of cognitive skill and proschool motivation.

Academic ability is a liberating factor for a child or adolescent. The greater a student's "pure" ability, the easier it is for him or her to meet the basic academic demands of schooling and thereby achieve school success. Students with marginal ability have less latitude in school because they must be better organized and motivated to meet those basic criteria of academic mastery that are required for school success. The question is not simply who can succeed, or even how much cognitive ability is necessary for school success. Rather, the questions are: What is the probability of success at different levels of ability? How much flexibility in the more purely *social* aspects of behavior in schools is afforded the child or adolescent who demonstrates a high level of cognitive ability, as opposed to the child or adolescent who displays only a moderate or low level of such ability?

What are the odds of success? Consider a study by Wolfe of American students in the late 1950s.[25] These data relate the probability (odds) of a person reaching a certain level of school success (educational attainment) at different levels of cognitive-performance ability (as measured by IQ scores). In 1960 a "smart" student (one with IQ higher than 120) had nearly twice the likelihood of entering college (60 percent versus 38 percent for IQ of 100 to 120) and of graduating from college (51 percent versus 26 percent).[26]

However, the issue is not as clear cut as it first appears. Sewell found that when he controlled for academic ability, children from the top quartile of socioeconomic status were four times as likely to attend college as were those from the bottom quartile.[27] When the difference in socioeconomic status increases, the odds become even worse. Bowles and Gintis found, after controlling for academic ability, that children from the top 10 percent in socioeconomic status are twelve times as likely to attend college as are those from the bottom 10 percent.[10] De Lone makes the point quite directly.

Educational attainment and the occupational and financial advantage conferred by it are not simply matters of individual ability and diligence; they
are in good measure a function of where one starts in the socioeconomic
structure.[29]

What does this mean in the context of the present discussion? First, it
reinforces our earlier suggestion that school success is a function of
"social" influences as much as, if not more than, of strictly "cognitive"
ones. Cognitive-ability and academic-performance criteria may provide a
kind of bottom line for school success, but within the intellectually capable
group social factors in the enduring social relationships of the student and
the school are accountable for school success.

Many have studied the causes of dropping out of high school. For example, Elliott, Voss, and Wendling reported that most ("as many as three-
fourths") of those who drop out of school demonstrate cognitive skills adequate to do "passing or even superior work."[30] The influence of social class
in this matter is clear. Whereas only 4 percent of the affluent, intellectually
capable students dropped out, the figures for the struggling and poor intellectually capable were 20 percent and 71 percent, respectively.[31]

A similar story can be told for college attendance, but we will reserve it
for a later time. There is a great deal of flexibility in the system connecting
pure ability to academic achievement, and academic achievement to school
success. But the picture that emerges highlights social factors as determinants of school success or failure. Few human organisms are incapable of
at least a modicum of school success (*with the proper social support*)
because of some sort of "cognitive deficiency." Although this is encouraging in one sense, it leads us to ask why some children and adolescents
possess or receive the proper social supports, while others do not.

The Third Condition: Prosocial Behavior

The child must display an accommodation to the rules of social behavior
governing the school. To be allowed to continue to participate in the
school's academic and social activities, the child must meet the school's
minimal standards of conduct. Thus the social influences on school success
are clearly paramount. For those who lack the appropriate style and manners, the school can and does become a battleground. As the CDF report
makes clear, schools use suspension and expulsion to clear out the
aliens—children and adolescents who do not (and in some cases cannot)
conform to a set of behavioral norms. In addition, most schools employ
passive modes of social control. Aliens may be "counseled" out of the
system at each important junction; students may be "allowed" to fail.

This is all part of the certification role of schools, a role that, according to Greer's historical analysis of schooling in the United States, has been central to the very *raison d'être* of public education from the very beginning.[32] Jencks puts this very bluntly:

> The primary criterion for certifying a student is usually the amount of time he has spent in school, not the skills he has learned. Schools do the sorting job that a meritocratic society wants done. Furthermore, they offer credentials that an employer can readily take to mean that a student/worker can take orders and fit into an organization.[33]

All this, of course, reinforces the ecological validity of our definition of school success. It also points to the political nature of any discussion of the meaning and origins of school success. Questions of class- and self-interest are at stake here. The point is this: Schools are primarily social, rather than strictly *cognitive* institutions. This point will reemerge when we consider the power of schools to shape student behavior.

The Contingencies of School Success

School success involves a series of contingencies or alternative outcomes in the process of educational attainment. At each point along this route, a passing grade is required for movement to the next level of educational attainment, whereas a failing grade severely diminishes one's chances of advancing. Our model poses the following question: How do the odds or probability of "passing" each contingency vary as a function of the social environment in which one faces the contingencies? Forces within the component systems affect these probabilities in a reciprocal relationship of *supports* and *stresses*. As the level of stress increases within one aspect of the human ecology (such as the family), its ability to provide support for school success decreases. As supportiveness in one system decreases, greater supportiveness (or relatively less stressfulness) is required of other systems if school success is to occur.

For example, as the organism's own intellectual ability declines (as evidenced, for example, by a low IQ score), the role of a supportive socioeconomic context increases. The impact of social class on school success is greater for those with lower IQs than for those with high IQs. Whereas an affluent student of low ability is very likely to achieve a moderate level of school success, a poor student of little ability is virtually doomed to school failure in the absence of some extraordinary external intervention.

Having sketched out this view in very general terms, let us consider it in more detail. There are four major contingencies of school success, the first two of which are inextricably related. These are *acquiring functional competence in reading, writing, and computation skills*; and *developing a pattern of conformity to rules of conduct*. These tasks merge into the agenda of the elementary school.

In a sense, the U.S. elementary school conducts its evaluation along a simple continuum of good behavior. Parsons reached the same conclusion: Elementary schools grade students on the basis of their "relative excellence in living up to the expectations imposed by the teacher as an agent of the adult society."[34] The directly cognitive challenges posed in elementary school are minimal. At stake is the ability of the student to develop some basic academic competence. Virtually all students can meet these criteria. The elementary school is a preliminary screening for the extreme deviants—the seriously defective organisms and the most culturally alienated.

The junior high school imposes another level of evaluation. Armstrong found that 45 percent of students with good elementary-school records produced fair or poor work in junior high school, whereas very few with poor grades in elementary school improved.[35] Finger and Silverman confirmed these results in their own data.[36] *School failure is a cumulative process: The failures are identified and weeded out at each step of the experience of schooling* (although recent expansions of the equivalency diploma have altered this somewhat by permitting failures to get back on the track). The junior high school plays a very important role in this process. By the time students reach junior high, the academic-competence gap between successful and unsuccessful students reaches a point at which students can be segregated reliably on the basis of performance, with significant effect. The junior high school raises the ante in the credentials game by demanding greater cognitive abilities, proficiency in basic academic skills, and a higher order of socially valued personality characteristics.

Finger and Silverman conducted a study of academic performance in junior high school.[37] They related performance to prior academic proficiency and to the expression of several aspects of the *social* components of being a "good student" in its various senses. They found that at every level of elementary-school achievement (using letter grades as the index), students whose academic performance in junior high school was worse than in elementary school were those youngsters with significantly lower scores on measures of "persistence," "self-control," and "deliberateness." These data suggest that the students who are not holding their own in junior high school are those who do not have the approved attitudes about school work. As one might expect, these "correct" attitudes are more important for the success of the poor than they are for the rich, more important for the "slow" than they are for the "bright."

The third contingency is the acquisition of high-school credentials— that is, graduation with training appropriate to either further academic opportunity or vocational placement. In the contemporary United States, high-school graduation has become almost a prerequisite for full personhood.

The fourth contingency is the acquisition of college credentials leading to professional and other white-collar opportunities. College credentials have taken the place occupied by high-school credentials some thirty years ago as a prime determinant of placement in the "clean" occupations of middle-class respectability. The resolution of these four contingencies is, in a sense, the dependent variable for an analysis of school success. These alternative routes tend to produce cumulative effects; that is, successful resolution of an advanced contingency implies successful resolution of the less advanced.

Graduation from high school implies minimal competence in the basic academic and social skills demanded by the elementary school. The rise of the high-school-equivalency exam (allowing one to demonstrate his or her academic skills through examination) is testimony to the fact that attainment of secondary-school credentials is coming to be viewed as so essential as to be a basic "right" of the citizenry.[38] Interestingly enough, we are witnessing the rise of equivalency programs at the college level (for example, the New York State Regents External Degree Program and the open-admissions concept for public colleges). Differentiation among schools and colleges in terms of the impact of the credentials they offer on the recipient's life (their "relative value") is a prime illustration of the primacy of social (as opposed to cognitive) factors in the origins and consequences of school success.

This chapter has examined the developmental contingencies involved in the origins of school success. A number of important ideological issues are powerfully implicated in the definition of and response to these developmental contingencies. Chief among them is the issue embedded in the conflict between the conservative/ meritocratic and the progressive/egalitarian responses to the question, "Why do some succeed in school while others fail?" The American history of "blaming the victim" reveals itself here as elsewhere, despite the upsurge of progressive policy and rhetoric.

The three fundamental (nearly self-evident but often ignored) conditions for school success are these:

1. The child must be allowed to attend school.
2. The child must attend to and process academic information.
3. The child must display an accommodation to the rules of social behavior governing the school.

We often fail to meet these minimal necessary conditions.

The phenomenon of school success may be expressed as a series of four contingencies, two dealing with the elementary school and the other two with secondary and postsecondary schooling. These contingencies function as a screening process. They introduce new methods and criteria for weeding out students at critical junctures in the experiences of schooling (most notably the transition from elementary to junior high school, graduation from high school, and completion of a postsecondary-school experience). Having set forth these conditions and contingencies, we can proceed to a full discussion of their operation in the real social world of schools and students.

Notes

1. For a more detailed treatment of these opposing positions, see J. Karabel and A. Halsey, eds., *Power and Ideology in Education* (New York: Oxford University Press, 1979); C. Hurn, *The Limits and Possibilities of Schooling—An Introduction to the Sociology of Education* (Boston: Allyn and Bacon, 1978).

2. For example, J. Fisher, *Human Intelligence* (New York: G.P. Putnam's Sons, 1976); S. Scarr-Salapatek, "Unknowns in the I.Q. Equation: A Review of Three Monographs," *Science* 174 (1971):1223-1228; E. Brody and N. Brody, *Intelligence, Nature and Consequences* (New York: Academic Press, 1976).

3. For example, A. Aquirre, "Intelligence Testing and Chicanos: A Quality of Life Issue," *Social Problems* 27 (1979):186-195; D. McClelland, "Testing for Competence Rather than for Intelligence," *American Psychologist* 28 (1973):1-14.

4. For example, N. Glazer, *Affirmative Discrimination: Ethnic Inequality and Public Policy* (New York: Basic Books, 1975); B. Gross, *Discrimination in Reverse: Is Turnabout Fair Play?* (New York: New York University Press, 1978); J. Feagin, *Discrimination American Style: Institutional Racism and Sexism* (Englewood Cliffs, N.J.: Prentice-Hall, 1978); D. Maquire, *A New American Justice: Ending the White Male Monopolies* (Garden City, N.Y.: Doubleday, 1980).

5. P. Slater, *The Pursuit of Loneliness: American Culture at the Breaking Point* (Boston: Beacon Press, 1970).

6. C. Greer, *The Great School Legend: A Revisionist Interpretation of American Public Education* (New York: Basic Books, 1972).

7. M. Mead, "The School in American Culture," in *Education, Economy and Society: A Reader in the Sociology of Education*, ed. A. Halsey, J. Floud, and C. Anderson (New York: Free Press, 1961).

8. W. Kessen, ed., *Children in China* (New Haven, Conn.: Yale University Press, 1975).

9. U. Bronfenbrenner, *Is Early Intervention Effective?* Washington, D.C.: U.S. Department of Health, Education and Welfare, 1974).

10. J. Hunt, *Intelligence and Experience* (New York: Ronald Press Company, 1961).

11. Recent evidence suggests that Head Start did make some enduring differences in the lives of the children involved. However, the verdict is still not in. For views from both sides of the issue, see Bronfenbrenner, *Is Early Intervention Effective?;* A. Rivlin and P. Timpane, eds., *Planned Variance in Education* (Washington, D.C.: Brookings Institution, 1975); Educational Policy Research Center, *Federal Policy for Pre-School Services: Assumptions and Evidence* (Menlo Park, Calif.: Stanford Research Institute, 1975); E. Zigler and J. Valentine, eds., *Project Head Start: A Legacy of the War on Poverty* (New York: Free Press, 1979); B. Brown, ed. *Found: Long Term Gains from Early Intervention* (Boulder, Colo.: Westview Press, for the American Association for the Advancement of Science, 1978).

12. Educational Policy Research Center, *Federal Policy for Pre-School Services,* p. vi.

13. H. Kohl, *36 Children* (New York: New American Library, 1967); J. Kozol, *Death at an Early Age: The Destruction of the Hearts and Minds of Negro Children in the Boston Public Schools* (Boston: Houghton Mifflin Company, 1976; J. Holt, *How Children Fail* (New York: Pitman Publishing Company, 1964).

14. R. de Lone, *Small Futures* (New York: Harcourt, Brace, Jovanovich, 1979), p. 177.

15. H. Averch et al., *How Effective is Schooling? A Critical Review of Research* (Englewood Cliffs, N.J.: Educational Technology Publications, 1974); C. Jencks, *Inequality: A Reassessment of the Effect of Family and Schooling in America* (New York: Basic Books, 1972); S. Boocock, *An Introduction to the Sociology of Learning* (Boston: Houghton Mifflin Company, 1971); J. Mincer, *Schooling, Experience and Earnings* (New York: Columbia University Press, 1974).

16. Children's Defense Fund, *Children Out of School in America* (Washington, D.C.: Children's Defense Fund, 1974).

17. Ibid., p. 3.

18. Ibid., p. 6.

19. E. Herzog, C. Newcomb, and I. Cisin, "Double Deprivation: The Less They Have the Less They Learn," in *A Report on Longitudinal Evaluations of Preschool Programs* (Washington, D.C.: Office of Child Development, 1972).

20. Children's Defense Fund, *Children Out of School,* p. 38.

21. R. Wolf, "The Identification and Measurement of Environmental Process Variables Related to Intelligence," (Ph.D. diss., University of Chicago, 1964).

22. Children's Defense Fund, *Children Out of School.*

23. J. Garbarino, "A Preliminary Study of Some Ecological Correlates of Child Abuse: The Impact of Socioeconomic Stress on Mothers," *Child Development* 47 (1976):178-185; J. Garbarino, "The Family: A School for Living," *National Elementary School Principal* 55 (1976):66-70.

24. N. Hobbs, *Issues in the Classification of Children: A Sourcebook on Categories, Labels and Their Consequences* (San Francisco: Jossey-Bass, 1975).

25. D. Wolfe, "Educational Opportunity, Measured Intelligence and Social Background," in *Education, Economy and Society,* ed. Halsey, Floud, and Anderson.

26. Ibid.

27. W. Sewall, "Inequality of Opportunity for Higher Education," *American Sociological Review* 36 (1971):793-806.

28. S. Bowles and H. Gintis, "I.Q. in the U.S. Class Structure," in *Power and Ideology in Education,* ed. J. Karabel and A. Halsey (New York: Oxford University Press, 1979).

29. de Lone, *Small Futures,* p. 104.

30. D. Elliot, H. Voss, and A. Wendling, "Capable Dropouts and the Social Milieu of the High School," *Journal of Educational Research* 60 (1966): 180-186.

31. Ibid.

32. Greer, *The Great School Legend.*

33. Jencks, *Inequality,* pp. 135-136.

34. T. Parsons, "The School Class as a Social System: Some of Its Functions in American Society," in *Education, Economy and Society,* ed. Halsey, Floud, and Anderson.

35. C. Armstrong, *Patterns of Achievement in Selected New York State Schools* (Albany: New York State University, Division of Research, 1964).

36. J. Finger and M. Silverman, "Changes in Academic Performance in the Junior High School," *Personnel and Guidance Journal* 45 (1966):157-164.

37. Ibid.

38. National Center for Educational Statistics, U.S. Department of Education, *Digest of Education Statistics, 1980* (Washington, D.C.: U.S. Government Printing Office, 1980).

4

Success in the Elementary School

Success in the elementary school is considered normal—an indication that a child's development and motivation are proceeding smoothly and in a manner compatible with the dominant culture of the society. Failure in the elementary school is generally considered evidence of either some sort of cultural deviance or some kind of physiological or psychological damage to the child as an organism. To be sure, cultural deviance may reflect only some fundamental social injustice, such as ethnic, racial, religious, or social-class bias on the part of the school. And a "damaged" organism may be repaired or otherwise encouraged to function through supportive intervention. Nevertheless, these are the causes of failure in the elementary school. Because of the nature of the task presented by the curriculum (the mastery of the fundamental skills of literacy and computation) and the social situation (the basic interpersonal skills of group life), there is a *presumption of success*. All children should be succeeding; it is failure that we must account for. In doing so we are drawn to an examination of the role of "family support systems."

Keys to Success in Elementary School

The first key to success in elementary school is an undamaged organism, one with no serious neurological damage and no severe psychological disturbances. Damage to the organism tends to result in three kinds of problems, the first of which is diminished cognitive ability. A multitude of forms of damage can result in mental retardation, and even minimal damage can be critical if the child does not have access to compensatory support services. The second problem is some sort of "learning disability" that somehow blocks development of basic skills. These conditions are surprisingly common and often involve some sort of specific perceptual, cognitive, or psychomotor aberration, such as visual reversals, memory failures, or lack of eye-hand coordination. These first two kinds of problems lead directly to difficulties in acquiring competence in basic academic skills (the first contingency described in chapter 3). This is not to say that such intellectual difficulties may not lead indirectly to problems of social adjustment—they often do.

The third kind of problem generated by organismic damage has direct bearing on the development of a pattern of conformity to rules of conduct. This third kind of problem is often labeled *hyperactivity*. It refers to a very high level of diffuse activity, a reduced attention span, and generally unmodulated behavior that places the child at odds both with the teacher and with other students and staff. The incidence of these forms of organismic damage and the seriousness of their impact on school success vary as a function of the resources and supportiveness of the child's social environment—as a function of its habitability.

In addition to these directly physical forms of damage, a variety of forms of psychological damage can impair a child's ability to master basic cognitive and social skills. These psychopathologies, which include a wide range of symptoms, find their locus either in extreme sensitivity (and thus apparent inability to cope with the complex demands of the school as a social situation) or in extreme nonresponsiveness (and thus an apparent lack of communication and interaction with social reality, diagnosed in extreme forms as infantile autism).[1] But of greater importance than these organismic characteristics is the relationship between school and home.

School success requires that the interactional styles of parents and teachers be complementary. It further requires that the significant adults in the child's home and immediate environs maintain the motivation to develop competence as defined situationally in and by the school. We can call this complex of attitudes, values, and behaviors the *academic culture*. As used here, *culture* is a definition of social reality through values and behavior. Mastery of this academic culture is perhaps the single most-important factor in school success. This is a problem because the degree of consistency between family and school varies across our society. The quality of the school–home mesosystem is variable both across and within socioeconomic and ethnic groups.

J.W. Getzels identified the problem of the academic culture as a series of "discontinuities" between school and home.[2] In Getzels's view, one of the origins of this conflict is the fact that "socialization" and "education" have tended to be viewed as separate and distinct functions. Hence, the interdependence of family as educator and school as socializer goes largely unrecognized.[3]

We consider the academic culture to be a particular combination of what Getzels calls "value codes" and "language codes," the definition of one's relation to reality, both behaviorally and affectively.

> The language code gives the child the categories for structuring and communicating his experiences. The value code tells him what in his experiences is important . . . for one child, the codes learned in the family and those required by the school may be continuous; for another they may be discontinuous.[4]

What are the factors that determine this continuity or discontinuity? Before we consider the evidence in detail, let us simply say that modeling and ideology in the home are most significant.

A third key to success in the school is the school's commitment (in both practice and theory) to universal learning of basic academic and social skills. Few children are incapable of learning the basic academic skills. The key is a belief in and insistence on the realization of this potential. In practice this means a willingness to transcend cultural differences (of whatever origins) and to provide the support necessary to overcome organismic damage. As we shall see, "superteachers" are those who provide such a climate of support and confidence, even to high-risk students.

Where social policy and community attitudes support child development, even academically marginal students will master basic skills. Therefore, political and economic support for schooling is the fourth key to school success. Even more important is the overall quality of life for children and their families, because family environments define the context in which schools operate. An environment of low habitability makes their task appreciably more difficult, if not almost impossible. Thus the importance of the "quality" of the school increases as the habitability of the environment decreases.[5]

Although it has always been difficult to assess the relative importance of each of these four keys, the ecological perspective outlined earlier does shed some light on the matter. Where the organism is damaged, the importance of other support systems increases markedly. The availability of diagnostic and remedial resources within the family (largely mediated by the socioeconomic standing, educational level, and childrearing acumen of the parents) and in the community (largely a result of ample and well-delivered services to children and parents) appears to reduce substantially the impact of organismic damage on subsequent development.[6]

Willerman, Broman, and Fiedler undertook a study to discover the long-term impact of organismic damage on intellectual development in three socioeconomic ecologies.[7] They found that the negative consequences of retarded infant development are greater in poor families than they are in affluent families.

The investigators found that whereas 13 percent of the children of low-income families who showed poor development at eight months also showed mental retardation (IQ less than 80) at 4 years of age, only 2 percent of similarly delayed infants from affluent homes were retarded at age 4. Even among infants showing good development at eight months, some 5 percent of the poor children were retarded by age 4, as opposed to 0.5 percent of the affluent children.

These results are consistent with those of other studies.[8] The incidence of "poor development" is itself higher in the ecological niches that are socioeconomically less habitable. There is more damage among the poor, and it takes a greater toll in the long run. One more example may suffice at this point. Inadequate nutrition is, of course, a major problem of those ecological niches characterized by low habitability. In the United States, millions of children have suffered or will suffer damage to their brains as a result of inadequate nutrition to themselves of their mothers during pregnancy.[9] Poor children thus experience a twofold victimization by their social class, first in utero and again in the early years of life.

Thus, damage to the learning and socialization potential of an organism is a function of socioeconomic factors operating through the institutions that surround families. Because these forces appear to be the "key" to success in elementary school, the importance of the supportiveness of agents in the family's environment is heightened. Furthermore, the very same forces that *increase* the probability of organismic damage *decrease* the probability of compensatory resources. The interdependence of systems within the human ecology forms the basis for this insidious relationship, and the likelihood of school success largely flows from it. How do these forces operate on and within our educational institutions? What are the mechanisms of school success?

U.S. schools have much homogeneity in most of the obvious aspects of structure, goals, and format. Cole and Scribner demonstrate this in their comparison of cognitive development among those attending schools with that of those not attending formal ("Western") schools.[10] The study of U.S. schools commissioned by the federal government and directed by Coleman likewise points to the overwhelming gross similarity of U.S. schools.[11] These similarities allow us to speak of "schools" collectively and to consider the common elements of the "culture" of U.S. schools—the academic culture.

The Processes of School Success: The Academic Culture

Up to now we have spoken largely of family status rather than of process.[12] We may now turn to an analysis of "process" variables linked to school success. These characteristics, which are both affective and cognitive, are the basis of competence as defined situationally by the schools. In Getzel's terms, they include both "value codes" and "language codes." A list of these characteristics includes the following:

1. Fluency in conceptual language.
2. A hypothesis-oriented style of personal inquiry.
3. Positive orientation to written materials.

4. Willingness and ability to delay gratification based on the authority of adult requests.
5. Ease in manipulating symbols.

The absence of these characteristics constitutes what some have called a *cultural deficit*. A more precise and more rigorous analysis suggests the term *cultural difference* as a more appropriate label for the phenomenon.[13] There are other cultural patterns that, although not as effective in the social and intellectual context of the school, are nonetheless anthropologically legitimate.

The academic culture tends to be rooted in the value codes of adults as a function of their position in the socioeconomic order. Thus, there is a positive relationship between social class and the academic culture. This relationship is not invariant, however. This is the starting point for the assertion of Tulkin and others that this is primarily a cultural or ideological matter rather than simply an appendage to social class. [14] Perhaps the best way to illustrate this point is to consider several studies that examine the process variables of academic culture in lieu of or in addition to status variables.

Gross's study of two middle-class groups is a prime example.[15] Although both these groups are Jewish, one is Ashkenazic and the other Sephardic. The former group places a high value on intellectual development through verbally mediated interaction and conceptual language; in short, it strives to optimize the academic culture. The latter group downgrades academic development and the academic culture in general. The differences between children from these two groups, with respect to the academic culture, are as great as between any different socioeconomic groups. The Ashkenazic children are competent in the school setting (and its related standardized testing situations) whereas the Sephardic children (despite their affluence) do poorly. Nevertheless, because of their access to commercial opportunities and training in commercial competence, the Sephardic children can expect to replicate their parents' economic success. Class is associated with the academic culture, but ideology is the key to the phenomenon.

Jean Carew and her associates conducted research that shed some light on the origins and consequences of the academic culture and its relationship to social class. [16] Carew and her colleagues undertook a longitudinal study of children between the ages of 1 and 3 years to determine the degree to which "intellectually stimulating" events were present. Only a minority of the children's experiences were found to be "clearly intellectually valuable." These involved events that included four cognitive domains: "verbal/symbolic," "spatial/fine motor," "concrete reasoning/problem solving" and "expressive/artistic."

These experiences were related to the IQs (intelligence quotients) of the children at age 3. This relationship was the operational link between social class and IQ. That is, the extent of intellectually stimulating events "predicted" the IQ performance even if social class was taken into account. *Social class added virtually nothing to the predictive value of the experiences themselves.* Caldwell and her associates reached much the same conclusion in a study of the value of Socioeconomic Status (SES) compared with a measure of environmental stimulation in predicting children's IQ scores.[17] They found the environmental measures to be much more predictive of IQ than was SES. Scarr and Weinberg show that disadvantaged children adopted by advantaged families show large gains in IQ.[18] They attribute these increases to the higher levels of stimulation found in the advantaged homes. Many investigators point out that families within various SES groups differ widely in the kinds and amount of stimulation they provide.[19]

These findings argue persuasively that the processes through which social class affects academic competence are found in the encouragement of the academic culture (although later, in adolescence, social class has an independent effect). Social class and the presence of the academic culture are, of course, powerfully related. In this relationship, SES plays an ever smaller role as the age of the child increases; the role of people in the environment increases until finally, by age 3, the child's behavior itself has become the determining factor. As the child becomes the "cause" of its own progress, some momentum develops. The child's characteristics increase in importance from accounting for about 6 percent of the variance at 1 year of age to accounting for about 50 percent at 3 years of age; the percentage of variance accounted for by social class, however, declines from 30 to 7 percent.[20]

Why does the contribution of class diminish? Class first has a direct influence, whether or not conditions favor an intact organism and regardless of the availability of supportive caregiving. As other things become relevant—namely, the quality of social input—class is replaced as a direct influence by adults in developmentally enhancing roles. As the child develops language, which can be an effective force in generating its own development, the child's initiations become increasingly important. Development relevant to academic competence and school success is a constantly changing mix of *factors in the organism* (child behaviors, in the study by Carew); *immediate setting* (the stimulating interaction and modeling of social agents); and *institutional system* (socioeconomic conditions). Social class returns to a salient position when the developmental issue becomes the acquisition of high-school and college credentials.

Van Doorminck and his colleagues have constructed an instrument for predicting school failure that further illustrates the meaning and impact of the academic culture within the home.[21] This work is consistent with Carew's findings. The operational measures of academic culture—even in the gross form used in this study (educational activities of the mother, books used in the home, and so forth)—are a better predictor of school failure than is social class directly. Low socioeconomic status and low levels of academic stimulation combine to produce academic problems.

Problems are defined as repetition of grade; and/or referral for and/or enrollment in any learning disabled program; and/or letter grades of D or F in reading and math; and/or average percentile of less than 31 on test scores, letter grades, and curriculum level. This evidence supports the view that the odds of school success are conditioned—but not determined—by academic culture. In other words, 71 percent of the students in grades 1 to 6 with low academic-stimulation scores encountered school problems, compared with 19 percent of those with high stimulation scores. Likewise, 43 percent of those from low-SES backgrounds encountered school problems, whereas only 8 percent of those from middle-class backgrounds did. If we consider the intersection of SES and stimulation, the relationship is strong but not absolute.[22] Class shapes academic culture, which in turn largely determines initial school success.

It is the experience of cognitively enhancing interaction in the home that makes the difference. Scarr and Weinberg speculate that a child's IQ can be raised 15 to 20 points by enhancing the quality of interaction in the home.[23] This is part of a consistent pattern of effects that clearly support the ecological model of development. The "causes" of development lie in the human ecology of the child, in his or her enduring relationships.

To appreciate the impact of these findings, one need only note the results of a study of elementary-school success.[24] In an analysis of scores on reading-achievement tests administered to elementary-school children in New York City, these investigators found that the differential progress made during the summer recess accounted for nearly 80 percent of academic deficiencies between the children in schools serving affluent populations and those serving the poor. A follow-up study in 1974 confirmed these results, and similar work produced further evidence of differential summer learning. [25] In a large-scale study of Atlanta schoolchildren published in 1978, Heyns provides additional insight into this phenomenon. As she concludes:

> . . . relatively advantaged students learn at a faster rate than do less privileged pupils. Disadvantaged children, however, show a higher rate of relative achievement during the school years than during the summer. The gap between black and white children, and between low- and high-income children, widens disproportionately during the months when schools are not in session.[26]

Thus, although some children continue to progress during the summer recess, others remain the same or actually regress in terms of academic development. What accounts for this? The answer appears to be support for the academic culture in the enduring relationships of the child, both within the family and in its immediate environs. Let us turn to studies conducted in Great Britain for further illumination of these phenomena.,

Wiseman found that 94.2 percent of the variance in academic achievement among children could be traced to two factors: "attitude toward education" of the parents and "literacy of the home" (the role played by reading and intellectual activity in the day-to-day family life of the child).[27] The conclusion of the major government-sponsored investigation of the origins of school success was that variation in parental attitudes accounted for more of the variation in academic success than did either the income of the parent or the material condition of the school.[28] Some of the data bear noting. A series of "home variables," which essentially tap the dimensions of "habitability" and "academic culture," accounted for 73 percent of the variance in "backwardness" (significant failure to master basic academic skills) and 63 percent of the variance in "brightness" (significantly above-average academic development).

Another dimension of the support system for the academic culture is what U.S. investigators McDill, Meyers and Rigsby, refer to as "parental involvement in and commitment to the school."[29] This factor, the degree to which a parent actually does things to indicate the importance of schooling, has been found to be of increasing importance throughout the elementary-school years.

McDill, Rigsby, and Meyers found this to be "the one contextual variable which is a source of climate effects" upon the school experience of the child. The British studies echo this conclusion. The National Education study reports data on the reading skills of children whose parents took the initiative in discussing their child's school work with the teacher.[30] These show a significant and strong relationship between parent-initiated contacts with teachers and the frequency of reading problems in the children—the fewer the contacts, the more problems. This simple gross index of parental support indicates that reading difficulties are more common among the children whose parents did not take the initiative to consult with teachers, despite the fact that reading problems themselves would tend to motivate parents to take the initiative in meeting with teachers. Class compounds this problem in that lower-SES parents are often ill equipped to deal with the schools.[31] This results from the language barrier of professional jargon imposed by the schools as well as by the parents' low position in the class hierarchy compared with that of school officials. In short, even when they are willing, many lower-SES parents find it difficult if not impossible to communicate with the schools. Thus, many of those in lower-SES groups see the school as an adversary rather than as a friend.

An experiment conducted by Smith illustrates a potential avenue for parental involvement.[32] The program emphasized active involvement by parents in demonstrating their support for schooling. But it did so in a way that permitted every parent to be successful if he or she was motivated. It asked parents to listen to the children read; to read, themselves, in the child's presence; to show interest by looking at the child's homework; to provide a no-television time for study; and so forth. The parents were not asked to help the child with homework; instead, they were informed that the teacher would be checking on whether the child did his work rather than on how well the task was done.[33]

The degree to which the home and the child's other immediate settings sustain a pattern of interaction and ideology that generate an academic culture (and thus are consistent with the school's insistence on minimal competence in this culture) may well be the single most-important factor in the child's successful mastery of elementary cognitive and social skills. This is true of U.S. schools, as of all Western schools, and could be changed only through a radical revision of the concept of what a school is. There have been attempts to do this, but the results present no clear pattern. The early-intervention programs that have achieved encouraging results are those that have created greater consistency between home and school by promoting the academic culture in the homes of children against whom socioeconomic, demographic, and cultural forces have conspired.[34] A brief intensive program such as Head Start cannot inoculate a child against the absence of support for the academic culture in his or her enduring relationships. Enduring changes in the child require enduring changes in the human ecology of the child's life. The relevance of each component changes as the child develops, the focus shifting as the child faces the various contingencies of school success.

Academic Culture and the Peasantry

There appear to be cognitive, affective, and behavioral outcomes that are common to those who experience being part of a "peasant" class. This peasant experience does not support, and is in some respects antithetical to, the academic culture, which is generally denied both to and by peasants. One historian of school success, Colin Greer, sees this as a major factor in ethnic and racial differences in the United States. Some immigrant groups, such as Jews and Greeks, brought with them a nonpeasant experience. Others, such as the Irish and the Italians, had peasant laboring backgrounds that mitigated against the skills and attitudes underlying the academic culture.

As school success became increasingly essential for job opportunity and as the unskilled and semi-skilled labor market continued to shrink after the Depression and the temporary priming of World War II, so those groups "permitted" to develop and strengthen the social and cultural status of peasant life found that it came to mean low status and extreme vulnerability in the marketplace.[35]

Who are the peasants and those with a peasant tradition in the contemporary United States? They include predominantly blacks, Puerto Ricans, Chicanos, American Indians, and whites from those rural areas of the country (or only one generation removed from such settings) where the economy is primarily subsistence agriculture. These are the people for whom the academic culture is most problematic. The motivational component involved in meeting these contingencies is crucial, and its role in the academic culture cannot be underestimated. Minimal opportunity to learn the academic culture in the home can be overcome by a strong motivation to master that culture once the child does gain access to it (for example in the form of a preschool "enrichment" program)—if the organism is not damaged in a way that substantially reduces the child's learning ability. A very highly developed academic culture in the home can equip even the most-mediocre and marginally motivated organism to master elementary skills successfully. Thus, the affluent are destined to succeed in elementary school because they are most likely to be healthy infant organisms, most likely to receive compensatory support if damaged, and most to be born into the academic culture. At the other extreme, peasants are likely to be thwarted at every step.

What Can Schools Do?

There is some important variance both among and within schools in their commitment to realizing the universal learning of basic academic and social skills. Although the effect of the school may be small in comparison with the role played by the forces that directly affect the learning and socialization potential of the organism, or with support for the academic culture in the home of the child, the school does have some latitude in this respect.

From the foregoing it should be no surprise that the structural and programmatic differences among U.S. schools account for only a little of the variation in the academic achievement of children. Coleman's research reached this conclusion, which has become part of the acknowledged orthodoxy of U.S. education—even if people do not *really* believe it.[36] Coleman's study put the matter this way:

. . . one implication stands out above all: That schools bring little influence to bear on a child's achievement that is independent of his background and general social context. . . .[37]

This bold conclusion is restated, in slightly different form, throughout the Coleman report.

In terms of achievement and verbal ability scores, the report concluded that it would be incorrect to say that schools have no effect. However, what effects they do have are highly related to a student's background and the educational background of his or her peers, factors that lie outside rather than inside the school.

Just how much variance can be accounted for by the school factors studied by Coleman? The amounts are not large but are significant. For the elementary school, the figures vary from region to region and are different for blacks and whites. Schools account for roughly 20 percent of the variation in achievement scores for Southern black sixth graders (versus 15 percent accounted for by home factors) to 10 percent for Southern white sixth graders (versus 15 percent accounted for by home factors).[38]

Indignant rejection of these conclusions came from many quarters. The Council for Basic Education reacted by stating that "it is absurd (to be blunt about it) to maintain that all schools are equally effective or ineffective."[39] In the council's view, the Coleman report's findings are so counterintuitive as to be beyond belief.

Others have demanded that the schools do more, that they somehow fulfill their mandate for equality of educational *results* (as opposed to mere equality of educational opportunity). This demand raises a painful question: *Can* the schools do more? The Coleman report challenged those whose automatic answer was "yes." Others took the challenge more seriously on its own terms. Charles Silberman responded this way:

> . . . it must be confessed that the weight of the evidence runs the other way—that at the moment, at least, the burden of proof rests on those of us who claim that schools *can* make a difference.[40]

Can the schools themselves do anything, either directly or indirectly? The data present several leads. First, the impact of differences among schools is greatest for the poorest and most socially depressed groups.[41] So say Coleman's data, as Mood viewed them. Using the fact that the school factors were two to three times more powerful for minority-group children, Mood concluded, "It follows that school quality is indeed of great import, and expenditures to improve it are educationally effective."[42]

These findings are important. The less support there is for schooling in the educational resources of the home, the more the student's academic development depends on the quality of the school. Thus, where a school serves an affluent group among whom the academic culture is firmly established, issues of school quality are substantially less important than in areas in which the people are struggling or poor. The irony (and, in another sense, the injustice) of all this is that the quality of the school is most likely to be high in the affluent and supportive areas and to be questionable in precisely the poorer and distressed areas where it is most important. Thus, it is clear that for the student body *quality* means the academic culture, cognitive competence, and attitudinal and behavioral support for schooling in the home. But what does quality mean for the school?

The Meaning of School Quality

The quality of a school is in large measure a function of its ideology and morale. The relevant meanings of morale are incorporated in a standard dictionary definition:

> . . . the mental and emotional attitudes of an individual to the function or tasks expected of him by his group and loyalty to it . . . a sense of common purpose with respect to a group . . . a state of individual psychological well being based on such factors as a sense of purpose and confidence in the future.

There are two general types of causes of high morale. The first of these is what psychologists call "the Hawthorne effect."

In 1921, researchers investigated the effect of a variety of working conditions on the productivity of workers at a manufacturing plant (the Hawthorne plant of the Western Electric Company). They selected a group of workers to participate in the experimental project and consulted them often to learn their responses to the changes instituted by the investigators— varying the lighting, work-line organization, and so forth. They found that no matter what they did, productivity rose. Brighter lights, dimmer lights, unchanged lights—all had the same effect. It turned out that the specialness itself was the cause of the positive effects. The workers appreciated being the center of attention, being consulted and interviewed. People respond well to feeling important and to perceiving the special attention of significant others. This principle, the Hawthorne effect, is now routinely considered in the design and analysis of human research. A related phenomenon, the placebo effect, has also been identified.

Giving people inactive agents (sugar water, for example) has been found to have beneficial medical and psychiatric effects if the "patients" (and/or the staff) *believe* that it is some potent medication or treatment. Frank reviewed the evidence on placebo effects in social settings (particularly psychiatric settings) and found that the available research demonstrates alleviation of anxiety and arousal of hope as effects that seem to relieve symptoms and promote healing.[43]

It is tempting to argue that by understanding the Hawthorne and placebo effects, we can also understand much of what passes for educational change and reform. Indeed, a book entitled *The Process of Schooling* does essentially that.[44] The research shows that there is a short-term upswing in positive effects and a long-term return to the baseline (original) situation, or no differences at all. Stephens is correct in his analysis. The key is that these changes produce an artificially high level of morale— among staff directly, and among students either directly or indirectly through the change in staff behavior produced by their change in morale.

It is difficult to document the validity of this hypothesis empirically. Studies rarely are designed to test it directly. There is some evidence that the long-run level of morale is not a direct determinant of "productivity."[45] But this evidence generally does not address the present issue. We can note several pieces of information that do bear on the question, however. First, we may read the first-person accounts of so-called superteachers as descriptions of the power of high morale coupled with personal competence. These superteachers ordinarily came to teaching with an extraordinary background or set of ideals and aspirations.[46] They typically have succeeded in infusing their classrooms with their own energy, creativity, and insight, the result being a buoyant inflation of morale (and a concomitant increase in achievement, both social and cognitive). However, these increases in morale prove to be short-lived for both the teacher and the students. Once the bubble is burst by the social realities of the school and the student's ecological niche, the old ways of behaving and coping take over. In the near frenzy of high morale, one finds all that is possible; mutual exhaustion allows the return of all that is probable. This pattern appears not only in the individual teacher but also in schoolwide special programs that rely on some new curricular innovation. Recent studies and our own experiences give evidence of this pattern. The alternative-school literature (both popular and professional) is filled with warnings against staff "burnout" and suggested methods for preventing it. Such prevention appears to be difficult, however. The standard developmental pattern in alternative schools is (1) great initial success; followed by (2) general dissatisfaction on the part of parents, teachers, and students (after the novelty wears off); and (3) a slow evolution toward a more-traditional approach (if the program survives); or (4) termination of the program.[47] Very few alternative schools survive longer than two years.[48] A colleague tells of an alternative school with which he was involved, which at the time of this writing had been in operation for six years. The initial years of operation were ones of curricular innovation and experimentation. However, as the energy and enthusiasm of the staff waned, the program become more and more similar to its traditional counterpart. The reason is that it is simply easier to function that way. The idealism that fosters innovation gives way to the reality of survival. In the long run, it seems, classroom atmosphere accounts for little in terms of productivity.[49]

Another illustration of the morale hypothesis comes from Silberman's account of the "informal-education" movement (at the elementary-school level) in England.[50] This educational reform was highly touted and was imported to some U.S. schools. The research cited by Silberman indicates that it has done no academic harm to British schoolchildren. Although there have been "no significant differences" in academic achievement, the reform has made British schools happier and more humane places to be. Current studies generally mirror Silberman's findings concerning the effect of informal education.[51] It seems that children from open classrooms (the U.S. term for informal education) show little difference in academic achievement from those in traditional programs.[52] Although children do not seem to be harmed academically in open classrooms, they also do not appear to be experiencing substantial gains in self-esteem (as many early proponents of the open classroom claimed they would).[53] In accordance with Silberman's earlier work, most studies report that students and children in open classrooms have more positive feelings toward school and enjoy it more than do their traditional counterparts.[54]

This is all to the good, to be sure. The mechanism for this effect (as yet mainly the result of anecdotal and informal observation and report) is a matter of some interest. By way of explanation, Silberman notes the difference in teacher turnover in the British schools, 25 percent per year (as opposed to 11 percent in the United States).[55] He implies that this means informal education succeeds despite high turnover: "taking everything together, therefore, the success of informal schooling cannot be attributed to extraordinary talent or experience on the part of English teachers."[56] The data (and our own experience) allow another interpretation. It may be precisely because of high turnover that informal education can succeed. The Hawthorne effect implies that the specialness of the program for children and staff may be sustained for a long period by a high turnover—and may in fact require it for its survival.

This application of the Hawthorne effect may well explain why the experience of informal education may parallel that of the progressive-education movement in the United States. If we read Wallen and Travers's review of research on progressive education of the 1920s to the 1940s, we may be prepared for the reports that should soon be written about informal education.[57] Only the high turnover rate—if it can be and is sustained—may prevent such a replication. The short life cycle of alternative schools, mentioned previously, speaks directly to this issue. It seems that curricular innovation boosts morale only for a very limited amount of time, before idealism turns to resignation.

Is there any alternative to reliance on the Hawthorne effect? Can teaching remain as a career without making it impossible to sustain the level of morale that newness brings? Enduring high morale may be *the* key aspect of the schools themselves (coupled with teachers and students who know how to be academically competent), when it comes from genuine social importance and not from synthetic "atmosphere" flowing from the events of schooling.

This leads to the second cause of high morale—enduring superordinate goals. Superordinate goals transcend the interests of an individual and bind his destiny to the fate of his fellows. Sherif investigated the effects of superordinate goals on cooperative behavior and group morale.[58] His findings demonstrate that structuring activities to induce superordinate goals generates high morale. This kind of morale, built on collective responsibility and cooperation, is not the short-term, artificial feeling that the Hawthorne and placebo effects imply. Unfortunately, there is little systematic evidence to indicate the power of superordinate goals as sources of high morale in schools; what there is, however (mainly in the form of anecdotal reports), is encouraging.[59]

In a survey of elementary schools all over the United States, Weber identified a small number of schools that were successful in teaching reading to children in areas in which the socioeconomic background and absence of indigenous home-based support for the academic culture indicated a low probability of academic success.[60] These successful schools combined a series of elements designed to lead to good morale, in the sense in which we have been using the term: strong and active leadership, ideological commitment to the possibility of success, high expectations, and concentration of time and resources on basic skills. High morale and "inordinate success" prevailed. We must not overlook the role of the ideological components of these schools. They believed in the children. They had high expectations and followed up on those expectations with the concentration of staff resources necessary to translate ideology into tangible results. In this they resemble an American equivalent of the Chinese educators with whom Bronfenbrenner spoke—the probability of success as a result of adequate attention to mastery seemed obvious to them. They believed in what could be done and then did it. Although there are limits to this, given the restrictions on the authority and scope of American schools, it is in many ways a reassuring and impressive result. Such early skill development is the operational definition of early school success and is tantamount to a necessary condition for later school success.

The School's Mission

The second thing that schools can do, with the assistance of the social and political authorities to whom they are responsible, is to change their mission, to become not simply educational institutions, but rather more comprehensive human-development centers. Much of the variance in educational outcomes is attributable to factors not directly linked to the conventional curriculum. Therefore, we can change the school to encompass the development of those outside factors in the definition of its role—its mission. Community, family, and human development—primarily social and economic matters with political overtones—may be the principal route to enhancing academic development.[61] Since families are the key to schools, schools must address themselves to family development.[62]

Nonetheless, schools are not free agents. First, the schools' very identity as educational institutions derives from a maintenance of the academic culture. The tension this generates is nicely outlined by Stephens.[63] Second, the limits that political institutions place on the school's power and authority preclude unilateral intrusion into the privacy of the home, the workings of the community, and the individualism of the students. To increase the success of our schools, we may have to change our conception of what a school is, what it is for, and what its role in the community of neighborhoods and families should be.

Looking across cultures, we see that institutional systems (legal, economic, political, and ideological) are the most important factors in accounting for differences in the ecology of human development.[64] It is here, in the realm of social policy, that the overarching decisions affecting the mastery of basic cognitive and social skills are made. These contingencies are so fundamental to basic socialization that their outcomes provide a good index of social habitability in a modern society (in other types of society they may be much less important to the quality of life). Students of human development have concluded that the best way to know the fundamental character of a society is to examine the way it provides for its children and the people who care for those children.[65] When social disruption subjects families to stress, when support systems are diminished, children suffer. When there is a lack of wisdom or a lack of resources or blatant evil in the social and political governance of a society, the habitability of the environments of families declines.

The policies and practices of the major institutions of the society—government, industry, church, media—directly affect the settings in which children are conceived, born, and raised. Since the forces directing these policies and practices are the institutional structure and ideology of the social system, it is these forces that are the overarching factors in early school success.

Ultimately, these factors determine the probability that an organism will be damaged, and, if so, whether or not that damage will be diagnosed and remedial action initiated. They determine whether or not socioeconomic and demographic stresses will affect families, increasing the probability of family disruption and concomitantly undermining the foundations of the academic culture. Through their influence in board rooms, legislatures, and other centers of power, they shape the policies and objectives—the commitments—of the schools themselves. The priority given to the well-being and socialization of families is at the heart of the institutional-ideological system's role in affecting school success. The goals guiding these policies often have nothing to do with social habitability. Rather, they are often focused on capital gains for the vested interests to whom managers—political and business—owe their allegiance. This sets up a real tension.

Affluence may obscure the ranking of priorities, such as families versus profits. This seems true of systems in general, be they families or bureaucratic organizations. As a group, we in the United States have been relieved of the need to allocate resources as a function of priorities. This is the real freedom of affluence, in which our national character finds its roots.[66] Scarcity of resources highlights the ranking of priorities and exposes the role played by the ideological system in the way children develop basic competence. The retrenchment economy of the 1980s may make this point painfully clear to us.

The Impact of Ideological and
Institutional Systems

As noted previously, organismic damage is an important contributor to school failure, particularly among those living in poor socioeconomic conditions. It is difficult to find adequate data on the incidence of organismic damage and its relation to the policies and practices of political institutions. Data are available, however, on the incidence of infant mortality (death in the first year of life). For every infant who dies, there are many who are damaged but survive. The incidence of infant mortality is thought to be a reasonably good index of organismic damage in the early years of life.[67]

As Kessner reports, there is great variation in the incidence of infant mortality as a function of the socioeconomic resources and availability of health care in specific ecological niches.[68] For example, he cites the extreme difference between an affluent suburb (with a rate of 13 deaths per 1,000 infants) and a poor inner-city area (with a rate of 41.5 per 1,000). U.S. census figures indicate similar variation among the fifty United States. Whereas Utah, for example, reported an overall rate of 16.6 per 1,000 (1970), Mississippi reported 36.5 deaths per 1,000 births (1970). In these states, as throughout the United States, the death rate for infants reflects the socioeconomic differences noted by Kessner, as well as allied demographic and resource issues.

Several "process" variables link these macrostructural influences to infant mortality, but chief among them is the relationship between resources and the adequacy of health care (both pre- and postnatal). In "unmodern" states with high levels of stress—and in poor neighborhoods and poor families—one gets less care, and there are more cases of damage and death. Kessner's study documents this association at the family level.[69] Although we can eliminate much of the damage by providing adequate health care, such programs are often on shaky fiscal ground because of partisan political considerations.[70] The politically motivated closing of these health-care programs in the mid-1970s was a predictor of increased infant mortality rates in the affected areas.

How are the policies that create and discontinue these programs formulated? How are decisions to discontinue school lunch programs made? The policy shifts of the mid-1970s away from the supportive policies of the 1960s indicate that in a period of retrenchment the value placed on the social conditions of children becomes a major indicator of ideology and institutional policy.[71] One may note that in other societies (in Israel, for example) these "preconditions for sound development" are of sufficiently high priority to resist a falling off of economic commitment to human services in the midst of a general economic retrenchment, even in a war economy.

It was during the "war on poverty" of the mid-1960s that an apparent upsurge in commitment to basic developmental needs occurred in the United States. War is perhaps the most powerful provider of superordinate goals. In wartime, from the government's point of view, the value of human beings as "resources" increases (while their intrinsic value as beings decreases). The Communist regimes of Eastern Europe, the Soviet Union, China, and Cuba seem to approach the matter from this perspective. The socialist countries of Northern Europe do likewise. There is great variability in this area within the United States as well. Among states with the same economic base, there is a relationship between the public-policy commitment to "human services" and the maintenance of a minimum standard of living on the one hand, and the rate of organismic damage (as indexed by the infant-mortality rate).

A second example continues the line of reasoning and investigation begun in the first. As reported earlier, the proportion of children out of school is an indicator of the degree to which there is support for schooling. As the data presented earlier showed, this proportion is substantially higher for children who come from families that are poor and uneducated. This association is comprehensible given the findings of the Children's Defense Fund (CDF) study about the reasons for children being out of school. These reasons include barriers to attendance for those who are deviant and/or do not have the socioeconomic and organizational resources to meet "preconditions for attendance," such as fees. It is clear that the forces that hold children in schools are less likely to be present in socioeconomically depressed and psychologically disorganized families. Once again, however, it is useful to examine differences among the fifty United States for an insight into the role of institutional policy in "allowing" these natural differences to exist and to have effects on schooling.

The percentage of children and adolescents (between the ages of 7 and 17) not attending school (according to the 1970 census reports) varies from 7.8 percent in Mississippi to 2.4 percent in Minnesota. As the CDF report notes, the rate is higher for areas that have poorer, less well educated people; have more nonwhites; are either very rural or have a large inner-city population; and have many children and adolescents living either alone or with one parent.[72] These are the basic conditions that seem to be associated with children out of school. What about public-policy concerns?

One way to address this question is to examine the role of state educational policy and institutional support, while accounting for differences among the states on the level of socioeconomic development. A preliminary study of this sort reported a small but significant relationship: As the level of institutional and policy support declined, the proportion of children and adolescents out of school increased.[73] Hence, there is more to schooling than simply the quality of the students. These relationships were found to be strongest for the poorer states. This conforms to our emerging conclusion that just as informal support systems count for more among low-income families, so also do policy matters count most in the absence of affluence.

To put this discussion in an appropriate national and historical context, we should note several basic features of spending for education in the United States.

Consider, for example, the National Center for Educational Statistics (NCES) cost analysis of U.S. schooling, which lists the total expenditures for public elementary and secondary education in 1978-1979 at $84.9 billion.[74] The average per-pupil expenditure during the same year was $1,900 per year. About 56 percent of the total goes to instruction and another 5 percent to administration; the remaining funds are for plant maintenance, capital outlay, interest on school debt, and so on.[75] Consider also that the center reported that 60 to 80 percent of local school budgets are for salaries.[76] Add to this the finding that these investments do not appear to be related to the outcome measures of interest—the complex of behaviors we are calling school success.[77]

In the 1980s people are increasingly beginning to ask questions. Is it worth it? Are the schools better for it? Are we as a society and as individual taxpayers getting our money's worth? The net result of all that increased spending is inconclusive. Since we hardly know what we *want* to buy, we can hardly know *how* to buy it, particularly since it is not at all clear that it is for sale.

Notes

1. W. Rhodes, *Emotionally Disturbed and Deviant Children: New Views and Approaches* (Englewood Cliffs, N.J.: Prentice-Hall, 1978); L. Hersov and M. Berger, ed., *Aggression and Anti-Social Behavior in Childhood and Adolescence* (New York: Pergamon Press, 1978); N. Long, *Conflict in the Classroom: The Education of Emotionally Disturbed Children* (Belmont, Calif.: Wadsworth Publishing Company, 1976); M. Erickson, *Child Psychopathology: Assessment, Etiology and Treatment* (Englewood Cliffs, N.J.: Prentice-Hall, 1978); L. Wing, ed., *Early Childhood Autism: Clinical, Educational and Social Aspects* (New York: Pergamon Press, 1976).

2. J.W. Getzels, "Socialization and Education: A Note on Discontinuities," *Teachers College Record* 76 (1974):218-225.

3. Ibid.

4. Ibid., p. 220.

5. J. Coleman et al., *Equality of Educational Opportunity* (Washington, D.C.: U.S. Government Printing Office, 1966).

6. L. Willerman, S. Broman, and M. Fiedler, "Infant Development, Preschool I.Q. and Social Class," *Child Development* 41 (1970):69-77; L. Willerman, "Biosocial Influences on Human Development," *American Journal of Orthopsychiatry* 42 (1972):451-462.

7. Willerman, Broman, and Fiedler, "Infant Development."

8. M. Winick, K. Katchadurian, and R. Harris, "Malnutrition and Environmental Enrichment by Early Adoption: Development of Adopted Korean Children Differing Greatly in Early Nutritional Status is Examined," in *Preschool Children: Development and Relationships,* ed. M. Smart and R. Smart (New York: Macmillan, 1978).

9. B. Newman and P. Newman, *Infancy and Childhood* (New York: John Wiley and Sons, 1978).

10. M. Cole and S. Scribner, *Culture and Thought: A Psychological Introduction* (New York: John Wiley and Sons, 1974).

11. Coleman et al., *Equality of Educational Opportunity.*

12. R. Wolf, "The Identification and Measurement of Environmental Process Variables Related to Intelligence" (Ph.D. diss., University of Chicago, 1964).

13. S. Tulkin, "An Analysis of the Concept of Cultural Deprivation," *Developmental Psychology* 6 (1972):236-339.

14. Ibid.

15. M. Gross, *Learning Readiness in Two Jewish Groups* (New York: Center for Urban Education, 1967).

16. J. Carew, "The Everyday Experience of Young Children, Observing the Psychological Correlates of Social Class and I.Q." (Cambridge, Mass.: Harvard University Press, 1975).

17. R. Bradley, B. Caldwell, and R. Elardo, "Home Environment, Social Status and Mental Test Performance," *Educational Psychologist* 69 (1977):697-701.

18. S. Scarr and R. Weinberg, "I.Q. Test Performance of Black Children Adopted by White Families," *American Psychologist* 31 (1976): 726-739.

19. Bradley, Caldwell, and Elardo, "Home Environment."

20. Carew, "Everyday Experience of Young Children."

21. W. van Doorminck et al., "The Inventory of Home Stimulation as a Predictor of School Competence" (Paper presented at the Society for Research in Child Development meetings, Denver, Colorado, April 1975).

22. Ibid.

23. Scarr and Weinberg, "I.Q. Test Performance."

24. D. Hayes and L. Grether, "The School Year and Vacation: When Do Students Learn?" (Paper presented at the Eastern Sociological Convention, New York, 1969).

25. B. Heyns, *Summer Learning and the Effects of Schooling* (New York: Academic Press, 1978).

26. Heyns, *Summer Learning,* p. 187.

27. S. Wiseman, *Education and Environment* (Manchester: Manchester University Press, 1964).

28. Ibid.

29. E. McDill, E. Meyers, and L. Rigsby, *Sources of Educational Climates in High School* (Baltimore, Md.: Department of Social Relations, Johns Hopkins University, for the U.S. Department of Health, Education and Welfare, 1966).

30. Wiseman, *Education and Environment.*

31. R. de Lone, *Small Futures* (New York: Harcourt, Brace, Jovanovich, 1979).

32. M. Smith, "School and Home: Focus on Academic Achievement," in *Developing Programs for the Educationally Disadvantaged,* ed. A. Passow (New York: Teachers College Press, 1968).

33. Ibid.

34. U. Bronfenbrenner, *Is Early Intervention Effective?* (Washington, D.C.: Department of Health, Education and Welfare).

35. C. Greer, *The Great School Legend: A Revisionist Interpretation of American Public Education* (New York: Basic Books, 1972), p. 92.

36. Coleman et al., *Equality of Educational Opportunity.*

37. Ibid., p. 325.

38. Ibid.

39. Council for Basic Education, "Schools Do Make a Difference" (New York: Council for Basic Education, 1967).

40. C. Silberman, *Crisis in the Classroom: The Remaking of American Education* (New York: Random House, 1970).

41. J. McPartland and J. Spreke, "Racial and Regional Inequalities in School Resources Relative to Their Educational Outcomes," *Social Science Research* 2 (1973):321-332.

42. A. Mood, "Letter to Science," *Science* 156 (1967):731-736.

43. J. Frank, *Persuasion and Healing: A Comparative Study of Psychotherapy* (New York: Schocken Books, 1974).

44. J. Stephens, *The Process of Schooling: A Psychological Approach* (New York: Holt, Rinehart and Winston, 1967).

45. S. Boocock, *An Introduction to the Sociology of Learning* (Boston: Houghton-Mifflin, 1971).

46. For example, J. Kozol, *Death at an Early Age: The Destruction of the Hearts and Minds of Negro Children in the Boston Public Schools* (Boston: Houghton Mifflin Company, 1976); H. Kohl, *36 Children* (New York: New American Library, 1967); J. Holt, *How Children Fail* (New York: Pitman Publishing Company, 1964); G. Dennison, *The Lives of Children: The Story of the First Street School* (New York: Random House, 1969).

47. T. Deal, "Muddling Through: A School Above a Bakery," in *Alternative Schools: Ideologies, Realities and Guidelines,* ed.T. Deal and R. Nolan (Chicago: Nelson-Hall, 1978).

48. A. Graubard, *Free the Children* (New York: Vintage Books, 1974).

49. S. Boocock, *Introduction to the Sociology of Learning.*

50. Silberman, *Crisis in the Classroom.*

51. R. Horowitz, "Psychological Effects of the 'Open Classroom'," *Review of Educational Research* 49 (1979):77-86; P. George, *Ten Years of Open Space Schools: A Review of Research* (Gainesville, Fla.: Florida Educational Research and Development Council, College of Education, University of Florida, 1975); C. Seidner et al., "Cognitive and Affective Outcomes for Pupils in an Open-Space Elementary School: A Comparative Study," *Elementary School Journal* 78 (1978):208-219; B. Day and R. Brice, "Academic Achievement, Self Concept Development and Behavior Patterns of Six-Year-Old Children in Open Classrooms," *Elementary School Journal* 78 (1977):132-139.

52. R. Horowitz, "Psychological Effects."

53. B. Day and R. Brice, "Academic Achievement."

54. R. Horowitz, "Psychological Effects."

55. Silberman, *Crisis in the Classroom.*

56. Ibid., p. 267.

57. N. Wallen and R. Travers, "Analysis and Investigation of Teaching Methods," in *Handbook of Research on Teaching,* ed. N. Gage (Chicago: Rand McNally, 1963).

58. M. Sherif, "Superordinate Goals in the Reduction of Intergroup Conflict," *American Journal of Sociology* 63 (1958):349-356.

59. For example, G. Richmond, *The Micro-Society School: A Real World in Miniature* (New York: Harper and Row, 1973).

60. G. Weber, "Inner-City Children can be Taught to Read," Council for Basic Education, Occasional Papers, no. 18, 1971.

61. S. Boocock, *Introduction to the Sociology of Learning.*

62. J. Garbarino, "The Family: A School for Living," *National Elementary School Principal* 55 (1976):66-70.

63. Stephens, *The Process of Schooling.*

64. J. Garbarino and U. Bronfenbrenner, "The Socialization of Moral Judgment and Behavior in Cross-Cultural Perspective," in *Moral Development and Behavior,* ed. T. Lickona (New York: Holt, Rinehart and Winston, 1976); U. Bronfenbrenner and M. Cochran, "The Comparative Ecology of Human Development: A Research Proposal" (Ithaca, N.Y.: Cornell University, 1976).

65. U. Bronfenbrenner, *Two Worlds of Childhood: U.S. and U.S.S.R.* (New York: Russell Sage Foundation, 1970).

66. D. Potter, *People of Plenty: Economic Abundance and the American Character* (Chicago: University of Chicago Press, 1954).

67. U. Bronfenbrenner, "The Origins of Alienation," in *Influences on Human Development,* ed. U. Bronfenbrenner and M. Mahoney (Hinsdale, Ill.: Dryden Press, 1975).

68. D. Kessner, *Infant Death: An Analysis by Maternal Risk and Health Care* (Washington, D.C.: Institute of Medicine, 1973).

69. Ibid.

70. Bronfenbrenner, "The Origins of Alienation."

71. Ibid.

72. Children's Defense Fund, *Children Out of School* (Washington, D.C.: Children's Defense Fund, 1974).

73. J. Garbarino, "Regionale Unterschiede der sozialen Wohnqualitat: Eine Analyse makro-strukureller Faktoren in den USA" ["Regional Differences in Social Habitability: A Preliminary Analysis of Macro-Structural Forces in the United States"], in *Region and Socialization,* ed. H. Walter, in German, (Stuttgart: Frommann-Holzboog, 1979).

74. National Center for Educational Statistics, U.S. Department of Education, *The Condition of Education* (Washington, D.C.: U.S. Government Printing Office, 1980).

75. Ibid.

76. Ibid.

77. H. Averch et al., *How Effective is Schooling? A Critical Review of Research* (Englewood Cliffs, N.J.: Educational Technology Publications, 1974).

5 Success in the Secondary School

Factors Affecting Success in the Secondary School

Since ability is secondary to motivation, schools *can* be effective in shaping the level of success among their students. The problem is to identify ethically acceptable and socially possible sources of strength. The key to secondary schooling is to harness the motivation of the present (the competition for peer recognition) and the motivation of the future (the transition to adulthood) and bring them to bear on the academic behavior of adolescent students. When we can do this, we can deal with the social and ethical problems of school failure.

Three major factors shape success in the secondary school. The first is prior mastery of basic skills. Given the cumulative nature of education in the United States, it is unlikely that one can be successful in the secondary school if he has not mastered the basic skills of literacy, computation, and institutional social relations. In this sense, elementary-school success is a precondition (although not a guarantee) of success in the secondary school. This is one of the tragic aspects of the trend toward automatic promotion through the elementary grades into secondary school. Such automatic promotion creates an academically hollow man, an incompetent student who will be exposed in a reputable secondary school (unless the policy of automatic promotion continues, as it does in some schools).

Second, success in the secondary school is affected by the social forces in the school that attract the adolescent to the school and to the process of schooling. The issue here lies in the social structure of the school. Does it draw the student into its activities and programs? Forces of social cohesion play an important role in the ability of the school to hold onto its students, particularly those adolescents who have not internalized the role of the student or whose basic academic skills are marginal.

Factors that positively define the relationship of school success to life success are a third condition for success in the secondary school. The secondary school is in many ways an arena in which present and future are in conflict. The social psychology of adolescence catches the student between a strong present orientation (the competition for recognition, status, and prestige among peers) and a future orientation (the recognition that studenthood is a preparation for adulthood). The successful secondary school finds a way to link its activities with both the present *and* the future of the adolescent student. A recognition of the role of the school in socialization to adulthood propels the successful student. That recognition may come from either the home or the school. The operative factor in all this is the provision of social resources to encourage and allow attendance. Discouraging barriers diminish school success, whereas support enhances school success.

How do these three key factors relate to one another? Unless the student has mastered the basic cognitive and social skills necessary for adoption of the student role, there will be great stress in the relationship of the school to the adolescent. This stress will revolve around the adolescent's difficulty in reconciling the dissonance between his identification with the role of student and his basic incompetence in that role. Gold attributed some of the motivation for antisocial juvenile delinquency to this struggle.[1] If the school is strongly committed to its conventional assessment criteria, there will be stress involved in any attempt to accept and define the academically incompetent student in a positive manner. Given the central role played by academic achievement in the ideology of schooling, failure generates strains in the student's relationship to the school. These strains, which derive from failure to master the basic academic and social skills, produce a condition of marginality for adolescents in their relationships to the school. This marginality must heighten the relative importance of the other key factors. As stress increases, the need for support correspondingly increases.[2]

Perhaps the most-important single element producing success in the secondary school is the perceived connection between the *present* activities of schooling and future prospects for life success. An adolescent who sees competent performance in the role of student as the precondition for successful transition to the roles of adulthood has the necessary motivation for schooling.[3] Ever larger numbers of U.S. residents have come to see schooling as the key to "the good life." It has the status of social myth, part of the "American dream." This belief is the motive behind the provision of the resources that allow schooling. Americans have been (and for the most part still are) willing to pay for education. This appears to be true across families, ethnic groups, and communities—indeed, across the entire society. Each level of society commits substantial resources to provide educational opportunities. Ideological commitment to schooling shapes this allocation of personal and social resources. The origins of this ideological commitment are to be found in many quarters. Among them are the fact that a technocratic economy needs workers equipped to handle complex written and symbolic direction, and that the political prerequisites of a republican form of government include an educated citizenry. But whatever their origin, these forces have generated a strong ideological commitment to schooling that has done much to set priorities for the allocation of resources.

This social potential has long been implicit in the ideological system but has been brought to fruition by the economic success of the U.S. system in the second and third quarters of the twentieth century. Greer documents quite well how educational success has followed not preceded, economic success.[4] Thus, communities and families have had to accumulate the resources necessary to support schooling, both economically and socially. Without this socioeconomic foundation, the probability of school success is and always has been very low. With it, the probability is much higher.

The importance of social forces in the school in attracting the adolescent varies as a function of the probability of school success. This probability, in turn, depends on the interaction of studenthood in relation to the role of adult and on the availability of the socioeconomic resources to support schooling in the home and community. When this interaction produces a low probability of school success, the social forces within the school become more important in determining the outcome for students. Conversely, high probability of success diminishes the role of social attraction. Thus, for example, the depersonalizing effects of large schools are felt most acutely by students whose background makes them academically and socially marginal.[5] So it is, also, that the poor and ethnic or racial minorities profit from arrangements that place them in a context dominated by students from affluent and majoritarian ethnic or racial groups, and in which they have the prerequisites to compete on an equal basis.[6] So it is that Coleman's massive study of the origins of academic achievement found that the quality of schools was more important to those students who had the least going for them—the poor, and the racial or ethnic minorities.[7] Coleman's study measured the quality of high schools based on staff training, availability of learning resources, and the like. These factors accounted for substantially more of the variance in achievement for blacks, American Indians, Puerto Ricans, Chicanos, and other ethnic or racial minorities than they did for whites, and for more in poor areas than in affluent ones.

Whereas the origins and processes of school success at the elementary level are reasonably straightforward and clear cut, at the secondary level they are much more complex. We can assume elementary-school success, but success in secondary school results from a historically defined set of circumstances. Secondary-school success can be understood only in an economic and social matrix that constantly changes as the underlying norms and resources shift. This explains in part why social policy toward education often seems so haphazard in its development, implementation, and outcomes. The context established by all the factors conditions the impact and meaning of each factor. For this reason, it is difficult to validate any analysis that attempts to shed light on *the* origins of secondary-school success. We can, however, examine some data to see how schooling works at the secondary level, and why it sometimes does not.

The Process of Schooling: How Does the
Secondary School Work?

Let us recall first that academic achievement is not synonymous with school success. The relation of academic achievement to educational attainment, although positive, is variable and only of moderate strength (accounting for some 30+ percent of the variance, according to Jencks's review of the evidence).[8] The strength of the relationship varies from individual to individual and from group to group. Understanding the factors that influence the strength of the relationship tells us something about the origins of school success.

The problem of secondary-school success is largely one of credentials and opportunity, completion of one institution's requirements and access to another institutional setting. This problem is set within the context of the observation that very few adolescents are cognitively *unable* to complete the academic requirements of secondary school. If this is the case, then we need to know why some students fulfill their potential for academically competent and successful behavior, while others fail.

The British educational system differs from that of the United States in terms of both its goals and its structure.[9] This remains true despite recent developments in Great Britain (most notably, the rise of the comprehensive secondary school) that have attenuated some of the differences. One of the major differences has been a much clearer and significant differentiation among secondary schools (high-status "grammar" schools, lower-status "secondary-modern" schools). The British system has been based on selection of youngsters for participation in elite institutions at the age of 11—far younger than is customary in the United States. This early selection and differentiation has been coupled with many more adolescents leaving school before age 17 in Great Britain than in the United States (on the order of 75 percent for Britain and 15 percent for the United States).[10] It is significant that we call these youths "dropouts," whereas the British call them "early leavers." An examination of the workings of this selective and differentiated system can give us insight into what schools can be and what they can do.

The British system has been characterized as one of *sponsored mobility*, in which the educational system selects youth early in their lives for future membership in the socioeconomic elite and trains them for that elite status. A system of selective institutions differentiates among youth and thus makes for a clear class differentiation among adults in terms of manners, association, style, and ethos.[11] This stands in sharp contrast to the U.S. system of *contest mobility*, in which socioeconomic outcomes are thought to depend on a continuing series of direct competitions. The British grammar schools's selective entrance is, in this model, designed to perform the socialization that accompanies sponsorship. Himmelweit and her colleagues performed a series of illuminating analyses of the operation of grammar schools in this role.[12] These studies examined the difference between grammar and secondary-modern schools. Their concern was with attempts to structure the academic experiences within the grammar school so as to promote achievement.

The underlying socioeconomic probabilities affecting school success are the same in Britain as in the United States: The affluent do better than those without the resources of money, position, and prior education. This similarity exists within an overall difference, however. At each level of socioeconomic status, British youth have been more likely to leave early than are U.S. youth to drop out. For example, 41 percent of the offspring of British families in the professional or supervisory category leave early, as opposed to about 5 percent from comparable U.S. families.[13] Within Great Britain, the analytical problem posed by these data is this: "Thus in the working class group, we need an explanation as to why some pupils stayed the course, and in the middle class group, why some left early."[14] Across the two countries, we need an explanation of why the rates for the two countries are so different.

This problem derives from the different needs of children resulting from the interaction of their position in the socioeconomic order and their level of academic competence. The working-class child needs more than tolerance and lack of failure; he needs encouragement, success, and acceptance. The middle-class child, however, must be discouraged from staying before she will leave.

Because the academic quality of the population bases served by grammar schools varies a good deal, there is substantial overlap between grammar and secondary-modern schools on the dimension of academic achievement. The long-range socioeconomic outcomes involved in meeting the different needs of middle- and working-class youth differ significantly. Himmelweit and Swift compared the lives of youth who were "overassigned" with the lives of those who were relatively "underassigned."[15] *Overassigned* means that a student was attending grammar school despite ability scores that would have put him or her in a secondary-modern school in another area. Those who were *underassigned* were youth whose scores on the placement exams would ordinarily have placed them in a grammar school but who, because of the high local achievement norms, were placed in a secondary-modern school. The comparison was interesting because it indicated something important about the operation of sponsored mobility. Being overassigned to a grammar school predicted twice the likelihood of ending up in the middle class than being underassigned to a secondary-modern school (87 percent versus 43 percent).[16] The luck of being overassigned carries with it a significant socioeconomic advantage because British schools are "strong."

Strong versus Weak Schools

Himmelweit and Swift proposed that schools could be distinguished on the basis of their power, with some schools being strong and others weak.[17]

> A strong school has coercive power over its pupils, deriving from the nature of the objectives assigned to the school and their salience for the individuals within the system.[18]

Weak schools, on the other hand, have little or no such coercive power. In the British system, grammar schools are, on the whole, much stronger schools than are secondary-modern schools because they select their students and sponsor them as elites. This phenomenon is illustrated by the socioeconomic outcomes of each type of school. The social-class background of the students in the secondary-modern school exerted a much greater effect on eventual social class standing than was true in the grammar school. Working-class students in the latter are as likely to end up in middle-class occupations as are middle-class students, whereas in the secondary-modern school they are only half as likely to do so.[19] Himmelweit and Swift concluded that weak schools accentuate social class differences. The key principle is that "background factors make themselves felt in a relatively weak structure but not in a strong structure."[20] This conclusion emerges from the finding that whereas there is little difference in socioeconomic outcome on the basis of social-class background for students in the strong grammar school, there is a substantial difference for students in the weak secondary-modern school.[21]

Himmelweit and Swift expand this analysis in their discussion of "streaming" (tracking), in which there is differentiation *within* grammar schools. The effects of such grouping appear to parallel the differences between grammar and secondary-modern schools in general. Streaming makes for stronger and weaker settings *within* schools, as does selection and differentiation *between* schools. Four grammar schools serving areas with different socioeconomic backgrounds provided detailed documentation of this phenomenon.

The major point of interest in these data is that although there is substantial difference among the four schools in terms of the background characteristics of the students, there is little difference in the percentage who left early (a crude measure of school success). The reason for this seems to be that the schools were able to engage in "social engineering" to compensate for their problems. Two schools have "student-background problems." School A has a "class problem" because it has a relatively low ratio of middle- to working-class students (31 percent to 69 percent), and school D has a "student-ability problem" since only 42 percent of its students have

IQ scores higher than 114. These schools became particularly strong through internal structure and organization in order to generate school success.[22]

School A selected students for the prestigious "A" stream (highest of three) on the basis of ability. This was designed to create an academically demanding elite setting. The school needed such an elite because the high proportion of working-class youth posed a retention problem. School D, on the other hand, had an ability problem and thus capitalized on industriousness in the selection of its elite stream. Schools B and C had no extreme background problem and showed much smaller effects of streaming. In schools A and D, a very high proportion of the elite completed school (84 percent and 86 percent), whereas in schools B and C graduation was more evenly spread across all tracks (with 56 percent and 39 percent graduating from the high track).[23]

The conclusion of the study was that streaming accounted for more variance in school success than did ability. Whereas stream assignment accounted for 23 percent of the variance in educational attainment when IQ differences in stream were controlled, IQ accounted for none of the variance in educational attainment when stream was controlled. Himmelweit and Swift concluded that strong and weak schools present different worlds for the student, and that the price for creating an elite is to create an excluded group whose feelings of failure may be intensified.[24] This last point is worth emphasizing. Power implies the ability to create winners and losers. Socioeconomic background clearly influences the probability of winning; powerful, strong schools can do the same. We now turn back to U.S. schools and ask, "Are American schools strong or weak?"

Power in U.S. Schools

One is tempted to conclude speedily that U.S. secondary schools are uniform and weak—uniformly weak, we might say. Both Coleman and Jencks suggest that differences among schools account for little, and background characteristics for quite a bit.[25] Let this be tempered immediately by a reminder that we are concerned with educational attainment—our operational definition of school success—not simply with academic achievement. Although academic achievement may not be particularly malleable, overall school success *is*, as the British studies show. We need to identify the sources of strength in U.S. schools, because in their strength lies their ability to affect school success. In the U.S. setting there are two key phenomena: completion of secondary school and enrollment in some post-secondary-school institution. We cannot simply transpose Himmelweit's model of institutional strength to U.S. schools, however. We have neither the same differentiation among schools (except that between vocational and academic high schools) nor equally formal selection of students. At some points, however, we can touch the American system with Himmelweit's model.

U.S. secondary schools do differ on the dimension of size (that is, of enrollment). The impact of size on the social dynamics of the school has been noted by many observers but systematically investigated by very few.[26] Although a detailed examination of school size is found in chapter 6, we can note here that small schools appear to be better able to generate social forces that involve students and bind the student to the school. The social strength of the small versus the large school is found in research showing a small but significant relationship between school size and dropping out. Controlling for the influence of socioeconomic resources (because large schools tend to be in more affluent locales than do small schools), the larger the school one attends, the greater the likelihood that one will not graduate. The relationship may not be large (it accounts for about 15 percent of the variance), but it has been found in some studies.[27] This is particularly revealing because in Coleman's data school size was not found to be substantially related to academic achievement (partly because Coleman's sample included almost no truly small schools). There is a great deal of slack in the system.[28] Academic-achievement differences do not exert a powerful effect on completion of secondary school unless they are gross and lead to some functional deficit on the part of students at risk.[29]

Tracking (the U.S. equivalent of streaming) is another example. Rosenbaum conducted an interesting and provocative study of tracking (or "ability grouping").[30] The study assessed the impact of tracking on intellectual development. Whereas most studies of tracking are difficult to interpret because of the confounding of race and social class with tracking, Rosenbaum's study is relatively unambiguous because it dealt with a school that was rather homogeneous—white, lower-middle or working class—in which tracking was comprehensive (across all subject areas) and potent (whereas over 80 percent of the college-track students went on to college, fewer than 5 percent of the non-college-track students did so).[31] Rosenbaum found that, across the high-school years, the intellectual competence (IQ) of the students declined within the three lower tracks and increased among the upper two. Furthermore, the variance increased in the upper two and decreased among the lower three tracks. Thus, the upper settings were differentiating while the lower were homogenizing. For example, the mean and variance of IQs in the upper college track increased from the eighth to the tenth grade (from 123 to 127 for the mean; from 23 to 48 for the variance). The mean and variance declined in the lower noncollege track (from 97 to 93 for the mean; from 87 to 78 for the variance).[32]

These findings parallel Bronfenbrenner's conclusions regarding the impact of socioeconomic and racial factors on the mean and variance of IQ scores.[33] Good environments and those implying intensive socialization tend to raise the mean and increase the variance, whereas bad environments and those implying more diffuse socialization decrease the mean and the variance. The greater the habitability of the environment, the more fully actualized are individual potentials.

In the U.S. setting, we can see tracking within schools as an attempt to inject the power of elitism into an otherwise formally undifferentiated educational system. Programmatic efforts of schools that do not somehow grab the students from a nonaffluent background tend to lose them. This is the natural pattern. It is the inevitable result of weak schools, but strong schools can reverse the pattern. Although we have little systematic evidence to illustrate the power of strong schools in the United States, we do have some informal evidence. The storefront academies (such as Harlem Prep) that exist in some parts of the country have in many cases exhibited remarkable strength. They are small, which leads to strength because it generates the social cohesion created when everyone is needed.[34] They are clearly special, and thus the Hawthorne and placebo effects noted earlier are invoked. They tend to present students with a high level of both support *and* demands, the optimal conditions for producing achievement motivation.[35] And they tend to use superordinate goals effectively to generate and sustain a high level of morale. Perhaps most importantly, however, they are positively selective. To be part of them is recognition of one's worth and potential. They are to the regular schools what the high tracks are to the rest of the student body—an elite.

Within the schools the power of social forces works to shape academic achievement, to pick up the slack between ability and performance. Of great importance in shaping academic behavior is the role of educational aspirations and the legitimacy granted schooling as an activity. Both Coleman and Jencks have reported that educational aspirations are a good predictor of actual school success.[36] That this finding is surprising to many of us only illustrates the flawed concept of the origins of school success that prevails in our society. Since most adolescents are capable of completing high school, it is only reasonable to assume that motivation is the key. As stated earlier, school success is primarily a social phenomenon rather than a cognitive one. Strodtbeck reported that nearly 50 percent of the youth from high socioeconomic backgrounds were overachievers (that is, had grades substantially higher than would be predicted from IQ scores), as opposed to 35 percent of youth from middle-class homes and 27 percent of poor youth.[37] This is a prime example of the slack in the system. Success comes from social forces, and those social forces generally act to benefit the socioeconomically privileged.

Damico studied the role of cliques in shaping academic performance among ninth graders.[38] This allowed some insight into the role of social forces in the peer group as an influence on achievement. Although the evidence showed that cliques were not formed on the basis of academic ability, membership in peer groups exerted a strong influence on academic performance. Damico found clique-group grade-point averages to be a better predictor of individual-student grade-point averages than were individual aptitude scores. As Damico concluded, "it thus appears that group pressure has led many students either to significantly over- or underachieve."[39] This is social force at work randomly. The essence of rationality is to put those forces to work in a prosocial manner through social engineering.

Data presented by both Coleman and Jencks indicated that the single most-potent school force affecting educational attainment is the level of aspiration of one's fellow students.[40] The certainty of this in the U.S. setting is frustrating to many who seek to promote greater social and educational equality. Where do these high educational aspirations come from? The most-general answer, "from the home," is in fact true.[41] However—and this is a crucial point—educational aspirations, unlike achievement or ability, are clearly a matter of ideology. And if there is one thing that institutional arrangements and the social psychology of groups can affect, it is ideology. This, it would seem, is the real opening for schools at the secondary level.

The problem is not, in general, one of inadequate ability to meet the basic skill requirements for completing secondary school, but one of ideology, educational aspirations, and the social support for those aspirations. As the performance of the children of the affluent demonstrates, virtually anyone can complete secondary schooling if he or she has adequate social support and ideologically based motivation to do so. Where school failure is a problem, we may consider social engineering that uses ideology in an ameliorative way. This may be vital as an adjunct to other programs of social change involving the schools (most notably racial desegregation) where the probabilities of school failure among some groups are higher than others.

In the United States in the 1980s, completing secondary school is primarily a problem for hard-core depressed and oppressed groups living either in extreme geographic isolation in rural areas, or in extreme socioeconomic deprivation in urban areas. Meeting the demands of postsecondary schooling, on the other hand, is a question of more-comprehensive application in the current social context, a set of conditions that shows some signs of having stabilized after two decades of change. Silberman reports that whereas in 1953, 48 percent of the top quarter of U.S. high-school students went on to college, by 1960 that figure was 80 percent.[42] By 1978, 46 percent of the incoming college freshmen came from the top quarter of their senior classes.[43] There was very little change in the attendance rate of the bottom quarter of the students. This suggests greater educational opportunity based on merit. It does, of course, obscure the facts that grades are only moderately correlated with intellectual ability and that the influence of socioeconomic background on grades is not simply through differential ability but has an independent effect. Strodtbeck's findings on "overachievers" illustrates this.[44] Since World War II, postsecondary education has become a staple item for children of the comfortable-affluent group and an achievable goal for the brightest and most highly motivated of the struggling. With few exceptions, the children of the poor have become increasingly isolated as their lack of school success has made them increasingly deviant. In 1972, 78 percent of the high-school seniors from upper-middle-class families went on to college, whereas only 35 percent from lower-class backgrounds did so.[45]

As McClelland reported, the rate of college attendance for affluent students of low ability was higher than for nonaffluent students of high ability.[46] As might be expected, the connection between successful completion of postsecondary education and access to resources of all types is strong. It results in the rich achieving school success most of the time (with little regard for ability), whereas the poor rarely achieve school success (even if they do possess ability). Nonaffluent youth tend to be screened out on the basis of performance, whereas affluent youth do not. Although traditionally there has been little interest and support for the higher education of less academically able nonaffluent youth, there are always institutions open to less-able but affluent youth. These institutions allow the affluent to maintain their hold on the sources of social prestige and affluence. They allow such youth to receive credentials and thus to maintain their socioeconomic status.

Rogoff provided some relevant data from the 1950s.[47] Although 83 of the youth who combined high scholastic ability with upper-middle-class status went on to college, the figure for poor, high-ability youth was 43 percent. For rich, low-ability students it was 53 percent; for poor, low-ability students, 18 percent.[48] Kahl confirmed these findings in his study of high schools.[49] Some 70 percent of the affluent students from the upper three IQ quartiles expected to attend college, compared with 27 percent for lower-income-group members of the same ability. Half the lower-ability youth from affluent homes expected to attend college, compared with 11 percent of their poor peers of equal ability. The most-affluent students in the lowest academic-performance group were more likely to expect to attend college than the least affluent from the highest ability group.[50] This gives an ironic twist to the idea of equality of educational opportunity. We should note, however, that developments during the 1960s (that is, since Kahl's study) have provided more opportunities for those of high ability but low origins. The tremendous increase in publicly supported postsecondary education (community colleges, public four-year colleges, two-year technical schools, and so forth) plus the massive expansion of federal and state financial assistance to individual students and colleges has accomplished this.

The impact of tracking on college attendance among students from lower-middle- and working-class schools reinforces the notion that among these groups (more than among the highly affluent groups) the structure of the school exerts a powerful influence.[51] These data echo those presented by Himmelweit. Some 82 percent of those in the upper two tracks went to college, compared with 4 percent from the lower three tracks.[52]

All these data speak to conditions in the late 1950s and early 1960s. The rapid increase in the rate of attendance during this period (reaching a peak of 45 percent in 1970 and leveling off after that) has come about, as was noted before, through a marked increase in the rate for the upper performance groups—the top quarters of the graduating classes (from 48 percent in 1953 to 80 percent in 1960 to nearly 90 percent by 1970, according to Silberman's 1970 report).[53] This implies that there has been much greater equality of opportunity among students with high academic achievement. This trend has had its greatest impact on the socioeconomically struggling groups. But the system of colleges and universities has increasingly come to be differentiated among the lines of the British secondary system. That is, although more students have access to higher education, there is sufficient variation among postsecondary schools to give their experiences very different social meanings. As Himmelweit said of the British secondary system, "A Grammar and a Secondary Modern School child live in two different worlds as distinct from one another as the worlds of manual worker from that of the professional man."[54] The U.S. system parallels this in its distinction between the college experience at an elite university compared with that at a two-year community college or a four-year nonelite college. These different classes of institutions provide experiences and credentials of differing values and social meanings.

We should note here that 75 to 80 percent of the jobs opened up during the 1970s required only a high-school diploma, according to the U.S. Bureau of Labor Statistics.[55] This must be so, because the basic outlines of the socioeconomic order leave insufficient room to accommodate mass upward change. As Aronowitz has shown, the economic boom of the late 1950s and 1960s reached its peak and was replaced by retrenchment in the 1970s.[56] There is upward (and downward) mobility for individuals and subgroups, to be sure; but more-major reorganization of the class structure through the evolutionary forces of educational development and upward mobility seems unlikely. What may be at stake is the establishment of an effective lower limit to educational development.

Based on what has gone before, it seems that for the United States the most-reasonable and most socially valid minimum level of educational development allowable is universal elementary- and secondary-school success. That is, as a society we can and should make a commitment to the universal development of basic skills (literacy and computational competence); ability to function in bureaucratized modern institutions; and the credential of a high-school diploma, indicating experience of the secondary school as a context for academic and vocational screening and socialization to adulthood. The experience of higher education seems to be best treated as a major, albeit limited, force to generate and sustain higher-order cultural, academic, and vocational development. This recommendation is a response to the problem of credentials inflation noted in chapter 2. As a society we need universal mastery of basic skills and the integrating experience of secondary school. We have explored the forces that will control the realization of that goal. It is a goal we have not as yet met. Perhaps 20 percent of the population at present fails to master these skills and complete the secondary-school experience. In the current historical period that 20 percent presents a problem, both socially and ethically. That group tends to be excluded from full participation in modern society. Above and beyond the personal cost of that deviance, there is a social danger. The danger is made self-evident, and the ethical issue joined, when we remember that the members of that 20 percent of the population (much higher in some schools, of course) who experience school failure come disproportionately from the "peasant" groups in the society. Moreover, the phenomena associated with that pattern of school failure—the resentment, the lack of modern bureaucratic skills, the vocational and social stigma—are all impediments to overall integration into U.S. society. Later, we will consider the implications of our analysis of the process of success in the secondary school for some important issues of social policy. First, however, we must look at how this social problem relates to school crime. "Schools out of control" is a major problem that touches a growing number of secondary schools. This is the subject of chapter 6.

Notes

1. M. Gold, "Juvenile Delinquency as a Symptom of Alienation," *Journal of Social Issues* 25 (1969):121-135.

2. J. Garbarino and G. Gilliam, *Understanding Abusive Families* (Lexington, Mass.: Lexington Books, D.C. Heath and Company, 1980).

3. A. Stinchcombe, *Rebellion in a High School* (Chicago: Quadrangle Books, 1964).

4. C. Greer, *The Great School Legend: A Revisionist Interpretation of American Public Education* (New York: Basic Books, 1972).

5. R. Barker and P. Gump, *Big School, Small School, High School Size and Student Behavior* (Stanford, Calif.: Stanford University Press, 1964).

6. N. St. John, *School Desegregation Outcomes for Children* (New York: John Wiley and Sons, 1975).

7. J. Coleman et al., *Equality of Educational Opportunity* (Washington, D.C.: U.S. Government Printing Office, 1966).

8. C. Jencks, *Inequality: A Reassessment of the Effect of Family and Schooling in America* (New York: Basic Books, 1972).

9. R. Turner, "Modes of Social Ascent Through Education: Sponsored and Contest Mobility," in *Education, Economy and Society: A Reader in the Sociology of Education*, ed. A. Halsey, J. Floud, and C. Anderson (New York: Free Press, 1961).

10. H. Himmelweit, "Social Background, Intelligence and School Structure and Interaction Analysis," in *Genetic and Environmental Factors in Human Ability*, ed. J. Meade and A. Parkes (Edinburgh: Oliver and Boyde, 1966).

11. R. Turner, "Modes of Social Ascent."

12. Himmelweit, "Social Background, Intelligence and School Structure."

13. Ibid.

14. Ibid., p. 27.

15. H. Himmelweit and B. Swift, "A Model for the Understanding of School as a Socializing Agent," in *Trends and Issues in Developmental Psychology*, ed. P. Mussen, J. Langer, and M. Covington (New York: Holt, Rinehart and Winston, 1969).

16. Ibid.

17. Ibid.

18. Ibid., p. 168.

19. Ibid.

20. Ibid., p. 175.

21. Ibid.

22. Ibid.

23. Ibid.

24. Ibid.

25. Coleman, *Equality of Educational Opportunity*; Jencks, *Inequality*.

26. Barker and Gump, *Big School, Small School*; A. Wicker, "Cognitive Complexity, School Size, and Participation in School Behavior Settings: A Test of the Frequency of Interaction Hypothesis," *Journal of Educational Psychology* 60 (1969):200-203; L. Baird, "Big School, Small School: A Critical Examination of the Hypothesis," *Journal of Educational Psychology* 60 (1969):253-260; J. Garbarino, "Some Thoughts on School Size and Its Effects on Adolescent Development" *Journal of Youth and Adolescence* 9 (1980):19-31.

27. Garbarino, "Some Thoughts on School Size."

28. Coleman, *Equality of Educational Opportunity*.

29. Coleman, *The Adolescent Society: The Social Life of the Teenager and Its Impact on Education* (Glencoe, Ill.: Free Press of Glencoe, 1961).

30. J. Rosenbaum, "The Stratification of Socialization Processes," *American Sociological Review* 40 (1975):48-54.

31. Ibid.

32. Ibid.

33. U. Bronfenbrenner, "Is 80% of Intelligence Genetically Determined?" in *Influences on Human Development*, ed. U. Bronfenbrenner and M. Mahoney (Hinsdale, Ill.: Dryden Press, 1975).

34. Barker and Gump, *Big School, Small School.*

35. B. Rosen and R. D'Andrade, "The Psycho-Social Origins of Achievement Motivation," *Sociometry* 22 (1959):185-217.

36. Coleman, *Equality of Education Opportunity*; Jencks, *Inequality.*

37. F. Strodtbeck, "Family Integration: Values and Achievement," in *Education, Economy and Society: A Reader in the Sociology of Education*, ed. A. Halsey, J. Floud, A. Anderson (New York: The Free Press, 1961).

38. S. Damico, "The Effects of Clique Membership upon Academic Achievement," *Adolescence* 10 (1975):93-100.

39. Ibid., p. 99.

40. Coleman, *Equality of Educational Opportunity*; Jencks, *Inequality.*

41. For examples, J. Meyer, "High School Effects on College Intentions," *American Journal of Sociology* 76 (1970):59-69; A. Kerckhoff and J. Huff, "Parental Influence on Educational Goals," *Sociometry* 37 (1974):307-327, D. Kandel and G. Lesser, "Parental and Peer Influences on Educational Plans of Adolescents," *American Sociological Review* 34 (1969):213-223.

42. C. Silberman, *Crisis in the Classroom: The Remaking of American Education* (New York: Random House, 1970).

43. National Center for Educational Statistics, U.S. Department of Education, *Digest of Educational Statistics 1980* (Washington, D.C.: U.S. Government Printing Office, 1980).

44. Strodtbeck, "Family Integration: Values and Achievement."

45. National Center for Educational Statistics, *Digest of Educational Statistics 1980.*

46. D. McClelland, "Testing for Competence Rather Than for Intelligence," *American Psychologist* 28 (1973):1-14.

47. N. Rogoff, "Local Social Structure and Educational Selection," in *Education, Economy and Society*, ed. Halsey, Floud, and Anderson.

48. Ibid.

49. J. Kahl, "Educational and Occupational Aspirations of Common Boys," *Harvard Educational Review* 23 (1953):348-366.

50. Ibid.

51. Rosenbaum, "The Stratification of Socialization Processes."

52. Ibid.

53. Silberman, *Crisis in the Classroom*.

54. Himmelweit and Swift, "A Model for the Understanding of School," p. 178.

55. J. Norwood, "The Job Outlook for College Graduates through 1990," *Occupational Outlook Quarterly* 23 (1979):2-7.

56. S. Aronowitz, *False Promises: The Shaping of American Working Class Consciousness* (New York: McGraw Hill, 1973).

6

Schools Out of Control

On 20 April 1977, the U.S. Supreme Court announced a widely publicized decision in *Ingraham* v. *Wright* affirming the right of local school districts to permit corporal punishment. The dominant response among the many educators who acclaimed this decision was that schools *need* the threat of corporal punishment to maintain discipline and order, even if they never actually use physical force in the classroom or in the principal's office. Why do teachers and administrators feel that they need the option of physical punishment? At least part of the reason, it seems, is a widespread and growing feeling that schools in the United States are "out of control" or, rather, that schools are being controlled by the wrong people and social forces. Many educators feel victimized by the threat of violence, by vandalism, and by a hostile and critical public. The most serious aspect of this problem is the feeling that schools have been taken over by forces inimical to discipline, order, security, and education. This is the real issue behind the hue and cry about school crime.

Public-opinion polls reveal increasing public concern about discipline and order in schools. Lack of discipline was rated as the number-one problem facing schools in ten of the eleven years (1969-1980) of the Gallup poll of parents' views of schools.[1] Teacher turnover is so high in some areas that only 20 percent of an entering cohort of teachers remains after five years in the profession. Costs have risen so fast that localities are hard pressed to keep pace. Strikes and busing accentuate the sense of schools being out of the control of ordinary citizens. The mass media report dramatic incidents of crime in the schools—a teacher is raped, a student killed, a student extortion ring exposed.

These are the extreme events that receive public attention. The more mundane and more pervasive problems of school crime involve the petty destruction of property and the personal insults that are part of day-to-day life in many schools. Such behaviors flourish in an atmosphere where pro-social influences are on the defensive, where there is passive complicity by the majority, and where students exhibit little self-control. These problems, rather than dramatic felonious crime, are the focus of this discussion. They present the most basic and most pervasive challenges to our social system.[2]

Schools Out of Control?

In what sense are schools out of control? The issue of self-control is currently emerging as a central concern of applied psychology.[3] At stake is the ability of a person to maintain control over the conditions that reinforce his or her behavior. Loss of control is a challenge to mental health and social functioning. To cite but one example, the maltreatment of children is linked to "lives out of control."[4] Neglect is a passive response, that is, the collapse of any attempt to provide adequate care. Abuse is an active response, that is, an attempt to assert control over part of one's life (the child) as an expression of a general lack of control in the other aspects of one's life. The extensive research literature on internal versus external locus of control documents the importance of self-control in overall social competence.[5] Successful interventions designed to restore personal control over reinforcing contingencies have been reported in a variety of behavioral domains.[6]

Of equal or perhaps greater importance in the present context, however, is the issue of *institutional* self-control. Do those responsible for meeting institutional goals have the ability to achieve those objectives? Is authority commensurate with responsibility? Just as individuals may resort to desperate and extreme means to assert control in their personal lives when they feel threatened, so institutional personnel may respond in an extreme fashion to the loss of control.

As a society we seem plagued by inadequate self-control. National goals are set, but go unmet. A host of socially self-defeating trends (including street crime) continue unabated, despite our protestations. This lack of self-control is dangerous. The problem of school crime is symptomatic of the more general problem of inadequate institutional self-control; clinging to the threat of corporal punishment is but one manifestation of this larger problem. The neglect and abuse of difficult students is another.[7] Understanding school crime requires that we first answer the prior question: Why are schools out of control?

The answer is twofold. First, we do not adequately understand the relationship between context and behavior. Second, we in the United States demonstrate a fundamental cultural ambivalence about matters of collective responsibility and group action.[8] These two inadequacies are at the root of the social problem of school crime. Because both reflect the interdependence of human systems, school crime becomes more comprehensible and susceptible to remedy when viewed from the perspective of the ecological model of human development outlined in chapter 2. For the present purpose, four propositions outlined are crucial.

1. *The concept of context-free or pure human development has no validity.* Issues of social policy and practice are intrinsic, not tangential, to the study of human development. This has particular relevance to U.S. schools because of their emphasis on narrowly defined academic development and their neglect of broadly defined social development.

2. *School crime is best understood as a problem with the social habitability of the school.* It is an indicator of the quality of life within the

schools and, indeed, in the larger society as well. Our individualistic, laissez faire approach to social relations blinds us to the importance of efforts to create and maintain a social climate in our institutions that actively promotes prosocial behavior. Rather than seeing the problem entirely as one of stopping school crime, we must see the importance of creating a social climate in which school crime will not exist. Currently, most schools are an excellent growth medium for school crime. In our analyses we must recognize that defining the role of the school goes beyond empirical documentation of what *is*. We must be able to conceptualize the *potential* impact of alternative forms that do not yet commonly exist (in our culture, at least). Historical forms may also provide alternative models relevant to present concerns. This perspective warns us against accepting the often expressed view that schools do not "account for much of the variance" in important outcomes. As chapters 4 and 5 showed, from the perspective of cross-cultural, historical, and philosophical comparisons, we find a high degree of uniformity in our schools. We can hardly expect those differences that do exist to account for a great deal of the variance in behavioral outcome. Nonetheless, there is evidence that existing differences in schools are associated with significant differences in the level of pro- and antisocial student behavior.[9]

3. *Like all significant human phenomena, school crime is a multiply determined developmental outcome.* It derives from the ongoing, mutual accommodation and adaptation of organism and environment. Many of the most important factors are those operating outside interpersonal dyads to influence and even control behavior. These influences, which may be termed second-order effects, include, for example, the impact of television on the interaction of parent and child, and the role of a teacher's presence in shaping the behavior of two students. The central concern here, of course, is with those second-order effects that shape interactions having the potential to become perpetrator-victim dyads. These effects are particularly important in understanding and controlling school crime because many of the solutions "obvious" to us, such as hiring security guards for schools, may have undetermined and possible adverse second-order effects on student-student, student-staff, and staff-staff relationships.

4. *A sound model for understanding and controlling school crime focuses on the intersection of personal biography, social structure, and history.* This confluence of developments establishes the context in which any specific proposal or event must be tested and evaluated. The "question" is always changing; therefore, any "answer" must be flexible.

School Crime as a Second-Order Effect

The foregoing discussion directs our attention to the importance of social history in creating the second-order effects that shape, even control, behavior in schools. When we look at the social environment of U.S. schools we see an insidious pattern of second-order effects that makes schools more vulnerable to antisocial behavior than are other institutions and behavioral settings.

The increasingly impersonal social climate of the schools encourages school crime, particularly in the secondary schools. The origin of this climate lies in the trends toward large schools, curricular specialization, and a narrow concept of the school's social responsibility that gives inadequate attention to "character development." Research on social climate has found that optimum environments offer

> a combination of warm and supportive relationships, an emphasis on specific directions of personal growth, and a reasonably clear, orderly, and well-structured milieu. These environments have a high expectation and demand for performance.[10]

Many schools fail to provide this climate.

The school's impersonal social climate results in inadequate observation and monitoring of student behavior. The key is the lack of *personal* feedback, without which the schools cannot function as support systems for prosocial behavior. The trend toward an impersonal social climate in schools complements trends in the social history of youth that cause large numbers of academically, economically, and socially marginal students to be retained in schools, where they may become a disruptive force.

School crime results from an insidious combination of historical trends that have increasingly weakened the effective authority of school staff, have divorced the school from the community, have created stress and incompatible goals, and have generally reduced the manageability of schools as social systems. The result is that schools are increasingly out of the control of those charged with the responsibility of dealing with antisocial influences. This is the climate in which school crime flourishes.

The four hypotheses offered here direct our attention away from the perpetrator-victim dyad (the typical psychological orientation) and toward the forces that establish the context in which that dyadic relationship arises and continues. There are two underlying principles in this analysis. First, the social rather than the academic agenda of the school has the greatest impact on student behavior.[11] Second, the key structural characteristic of the school as a social system is the degree to which adolescent peer groups are organized around prosocial goals, are involved with adults in structured activities, and are positively reinforced for cooperative behavior.

The sufficient conditions for school crime are multiple, and the vast literature exploring the dynamics of crime in general and juvenile delinquency in particular deals with them.[12] The school itself can be one of those sufficient conditions when it stimulates aggression, frustration, and hostility. The social climate of the school is more important, however, as a *necessary* condition for school crime. This distinction between necessary and sufficient conditions is crucial for both comprehension and intervention.[13] The necessary condition for school crime is a social climate that permits the perpetrator-victim relationship to arise (as a result of the multiple *sufficient* conditions) and to persist (through the apathy and/or impotence of students and staff). Our task is to identify the factors that bring this necessary social climate into existence. The crux of the matter is the school's ability or inability to function as a support system and thereby to provide feedback and resources to students and staff.

Gerald Caplan developed and elaborated the concept of *support system*.[14] In his terms, a support system performs several critical social functions that are relevant to the school as a social context, acting as

> continuing social aggregates that provide individuals with opportunities for feedback about themselves and for validations for their expectations about others, which may offset deficiencies in these communications within the larger community context. . . .[15]

Support systems provide nurturance and feedback, warmth and control.[16]

The structure, policies, and organization of schools contribute materially to their ability to function as support systems. These relationships are nowhere better revealed than in the role of school size in shaping social climate. School size is an excellent illustration of the processes by which alienation, apathy, and anomie (and their behavioral correlates) arise as psychological adaptations to a socially inadequate setting. An examination of these phenomena will expose important features of the human ecology of school crime.

Many investigators have examined the impact of size on the social dynamics of the secondary school. McPartland and McDill, for example, reviewed some of the evidence relating school size to school crime.[17] They focused on the mediating factor of responsiveness, defined in terms of access to governing decisions, the costs of misbehavior, and the rewards for desired behavior. In their analysis, a small but significant relationship was demonstrated favoring the small school. Plath reported a case study of a school that reduced the number of incidents of serious student misconduct from 120 to 9 after the subdivision of a large high school (enrollment 3,000) into a number of smaller schools.[18] Of course, such results may be attributable to the Hawthorne effect (that is, the enhancing value of any special intervention).

Other investigators have consistently reported that *large schools tend to discourage meaningful participation in the social activities of schooling and a sense of responsibility, particularly among academically marginal students.*[19] Why are small schools a better psychological investment than large schools? Social activities are critical to the social system of peer relations and, therefore, to the development of identity, as opposed to alienation.[20] These activities provide a potential complement to the academic agenda of the school. They permit a wide variety of students to succeed and thereby to develop a sense of involvement in, responsibility for, and commitment to the school. In the absence of this climate of widespread responsibility, school crime can flourish.

Dreeben made this function of extracurricular activities the focal point of his analysis of schools.[21] He argued that extracurricular activities provide a healthy and needed alternative to the classroom.

> . . . either the rigors of competition and judgment characteristic of the classroom are mitigated, or the activity in question has its own built-in source of support and personal protection, not to the same extent as in the family, but more than is available in the crucible of the classroom.[22]

Getzels noted a number of discontinuities between school and family. One of these is the difference in emphasis on "universalism" as opposed to "particularism."[23] The school is more objective. It asks "what" is involved, whereas the more subjectively oriented family focuses on "who."[24]

It seems clear that schools tend to be "universalistic" in that functional considerations are primary. The tension between universalistic and particularistic relationships merits consideration, however. Clearly, there is a basic difference between family and school in this matter. But the degree of this difference may be important to our understanding of the impact of school structure on the ecology of school crime. What are the factors that influence a school to emphasize particularistic concerns in addition to universalistic ones? School size is one important factor.

Large schools promote universalistic (impersonal) conditions, whereas small schools can promote particularistic (personal) conditions. What are the consequences? It seems that whereas small schools make reasonable demands on adolescents to adjust between universalistic and particularistic influences, large schools are excessively universalistic, treating students instrumentally.[25] This is clearly the message of Barker and Gump's research, research that generally parallels findings from a wide variety of social settings, such as work groups and play groups.[26]

In broad terms, school size can have an impact on the character development of the student.[27] Specifically, large schools tend to exert a negative influence on the character development of most students by depriving them of important experiences in participatory roles. Such experiences are essential for effective socialization to adulthood and for orderly social relations.[28]

Barker and Gump's group found that, although the larger school provides more settings in which students can act, there are proportionally more people to fill those settings.[29] For example, although the large school may have both a chorus and a glee club, it is still harder to get into either than it is to be a part of the single vocal group of a smaller high school.

The kinds of satisfactions derived from participation differed in small as opposed to large schools.[30] Students from small schools reported satisfactions that clustered around the development of responsibility, competence, challenge, and a sense of identity. Students from large schools emphasized vicarious enjoyment, being part of a large crowd and generally experiencing what the investigators termed a "herd feeling." The small schools encouraged active participation, the large schools passivity.

Importantly, Barker and Gump's group found that large schools discriminate particularly against marginal students, those who have difficulty academically, score lower on IQ tests, and come from lower socioeconomic backgrounds.[31] In the large schools such students were excluded from active participation; they were superfluous. In the small schools such students were genuinely needed to maintain the activities and functions and, therefore, were actively included rather than excluded on the grounds of their marginal competence and social undesirability.

Not surprisingly, marginal students in small schools were more active and displayed a stronger sense of responsibility toward the school and its activities than did their large-school counterparts.[32] The large school breeds passivity and irresponsibility as a student (and staff) adaptation to an unresponsive environment. Leaders in small schools do not include marginal students in activities because they are somehow "nicer." Nor are leaders in large schools inherently snobbish. Rather, the characteristics of the situations themselves make the marginal students needed in small schools and superfluous in large schools. This "psychological" finding is of social importance because school success has become ever more important for economic and social placement, as seen in chapter 2. Indeed, the inclusion of ever larger numbers of marginal students intensifies the importance of size. Moreover, as marginal students have stayed in school longer, the likelihood of their finding one another and forming educationally and socially deviant peer groups also increases.

Additional evidence is available from other sources to expand and extend these findings.[33] Baird replicated Barker and Gump's finding concerning rates of participation in extracurricular activities as a function of school size.[34] Wicker and Kleinert conducted a similar analysis, with similar results: Large schools were found to discourage participation in the social activities of the school.[35]

Since any discussion of policy implies financial considerations, it is necessary to digress briefly to the matter of cost effectiveness. The issue of school size tends to be associated with questions of cost effectiveness, on the assumption that larger schools are economically more efficient. Turner and Thrasher reviewed the evidence bearing on this question.[36] They proposed and answered the question underlying these discussions: What is the optimal size for high schools, given financial efficiency, psychological development, and educational quality?

Turner and Thrasher concluded that there is a size beyond which the economic virtues of largeness are not significantly enhanced, but the psychological costs are substantial. The investigators propose that the optimum size for a secondary school lies somewhere in the range of 700 to 1,000 students. Other investigators have argued for a smaller size. Rosenberg, for example, concluded that the best range is 400 to 500 students.[37] Within this range, we can address both economic and psychological economies.

There is a point at which schools become "large," beyond which the damage to social climate appears to be relatively constant. This is a crucial point because much of the research on school size assumes a simple linear effect, and often includes no genuinely small schools in the design, only *relatively* small ones. Such is the case in works by Burkhead and by Coleman, among others.[38]

The concept of optimum size addresses the question of financial efficiency, a matter that is foremost in the minds of many of those responsible for educational administration. A purely social or psychological answer (based on Barker and Gump's results plus the replications cited) would certainly argue for somewhat smaller schools than would a strictly economic one.

This is an important point, but even more important is the need to adjust any optimum figure in light of student characteristics. *As the academic marginality of students increases, optimum school size decreases.* As youthful alienation increases because of historical trends toward age segregation, stressful family relations, and disrupted socialization, the need for small schools increases.[39] A proper accounting of the costs involved in school size must now include its impact on school crime. Documentation that small schools can reduce vandalism, the need for security measures, institutionalization of delinquent students, and other aspects of the school-crime problem will enhance their fiscal desirability.

To recapitulate, large schools tend to promote alienation by depriving students of opportunities for participation in extracurricular activities. Such activities are precisely the ones that are vital in the peer-oriented social system of adolescents. This effect of largeness is greatest for those who are academically marginal and are therefore already predisposed to alienation as a response to failure. The structure of the immediate setting (the high school) seems to have an important impact on both the attitudes and the behavior of students. The issue is that of social identity versus alienation.

Large schools appear to generate alienation from academic authorities by inhibiting the kind of interaction that generates social identity, the integration of self, and group interest that leads to prosocial behavior and a sense of personal responsibility for the collective good. In place of such interaction, large schools offer undifferentiated collectivities. For students in general, but particularly for the academically marginal student, the large school produces a cutting off of allegiance, a self-protective severing of identification. The social consequences of this psychological response include a pervasive lack of collective responsibility, which permits school crime to flourish.

This is not the whole story, however. School size is part of a larger ecological "conspiracy." Structural issues tend to be associated with questions of size. Blyth, Simmons, and Bush, for example, found that grade cohorts in junior high schools (grades 7 through 9) were uniformly and substantially larger than grade cohorts in extended elementary schools (grades kindergarten through 8).[40] In the city they studied, there was no overlap in the distribution of sizes between the two types of schools. For present purposes, however, the most important finding was that the level of victimization (including robbery, physical beating, or theft in or around school) was substantially higher (42 percent versus 25 percent) for seventh graders in the junior high schools than it was in the extended elementary schools. Anomie was higher and participation lower among the junior-high-school seventh graders as well. Just as issues of school structure and size tend to be confounded, so also are school and community size.

For both the school and the adult community, bigness implies an instrumental and impersonal orientation in interpersonal and institutional relationships. Such an orientation is likely to generate alienation in both settings, city and school. Barker and Gump note this parallelism.[41] They found the school and community to be harmonious.

> . . . the small communities, like the small schools, provided positions for functional importance for adolescents more frequently; and the cities, like the large schools, provided such positions less frequently.[42]

Working together, the large city and the large school form a consistent human ecology dominated by impersonalized, instrumental interactions.[43] Both these systems alienate their youth. Thus, the problem of school crime is an ecological one, resulting from a "conspiracy" of large systems that preclude adequate personalized feedback and support and, in so doing, both stimulate and permit antisocial behavior.

The Ideological Problems Facing U.S. Schools
and Their Relationship to School Size

Why are schools big? Schools could be small but seldom are, for two ideological reasons. First, the emphasis of educational experts on primarily cognitive academic curricula has led to a concern for and interest in the power of large schools, their ability to provide diverse intellectual resources for students.[44] The lack of concern for the social issues involved in school size may have stemmed from the assumption that the primary issues were academic. This may have been true in the 1950s, when the major drive to eliminate small schools gathered momentum. An analysis by Heath highlights this point.[45] He reports that many states mandated the consolidation of small schools (400–600 enrollment) into large schools with enrollments in the thousands.

The development of U.S. educational institutions—indeed, of all institutions—has not operated under an assumption of high priority for smallness. There is a thrust toward bigness in the life of Western societies.[46] "Enrollments" in all institutions have been "allowed" to grow in a generally haphazard and unplanned manner, with little or no consideration given to the impact of such growth on social dynamics. This is particularly true of schools. Where planning has existed (for example, in the development of central schools), it has been in the direction of promoting largeness. The United States has accepted and even welcomed largeness under the assumption that big schools mean diversity, power, and opportunity for educational specialization and differentiation.

Clark points out that one aspect of largeness not usually recognized is the depersonalization of *staff*.[47] The result is a bureaucratization of staff relations and the concomitant need of teachers to organize and be organized.[48] A related finding is that large schools suffer in a generalized fashion by becoming bureaucratized and inflexible. The Rand Corporation reviewed the available evidence and found that:

> There is a positive correlation between size of system and degree of centralization. . . . Large educational bureaucracies and large numbers of rules *decrease* innovation and adaption.[49]

The bigger the school, the more change depends upon outside pressure.[50] The Ford Foundation, echoing this finding in *A Foundation Goes to School,* concluded that "Small schools changed faster than large ones."[51] They attributed this greater flexibility to the greater impact of individual effort, which also had the effect of making the long-term consequences of innovation more dependent on the continued activity and presence of individual leaders. Controlling school crime requires, above all, a personalized social climate. The ability to be flexible and responsive to change is an important attribute of the small school. Although this potential is not always fulfilled, it certainly seems easier to foster in an institution whose size lends itself to flexibility and responsiveness than in one whose size places it at odds with these goals.

Large schools generate and sustain impersonal systems of social control.[52] They resort to bureaucratized means for observing and reinforcing student behavior. At present, when the forces promoting prosocial behavior see themselves in jeopardy, this is unfortunate. Crime in general flourishes in the absence of personal responsibility, accountability, and contingent consequences for specific acts. School crime is no different.[53]

Winston Churchill once observed that "we shape our surroundings and then our surroundings shape us." Moos calls this the principle of "progressive conformity."[54] It is vital to keep this in mind because it cautions those who live and participate in "small" social settings (small towns, small schools, and so forth) to be wary, on the one hand, of too harshly judging their counterparts in "large" settings, and, on the other, of assuming that they will be able to retain their "niceness" if they allow their social environments to become large. Staff become inflexible, students alienated, and the social climate depersonalized in response to increasing school size. This seems to have happened throughout the United States during the 1950s and 1960s as small schools gave way to large ones. Recent research on the attitudes of adolescents toward their schools as social settings illustrates this phenomenon.

In the course of studying the adolescent experience of schooling, Buxton found that students resented school structure and policy.[55] They reacted negatively to rules, passes, and schedules.[56] This finding is from schools in suburban, mainly middle- and upper-middle-class communities. As such it represents the typical pattern of depersonalization engendered in large suburban (and urban) schools.[57] Student responses to the specifics of academic life are clearly negative. A recent New York State Commission on Education commissioned a study of student alienation.[58] This study indicates that, statewide, *"50 percent of the students will either drop out physically or remain in school as a mental drop-out."*[59] [emphasis added]

The essential criterion for evaluating schools is the "match" of social climate to student characteristics. Where the students' intrinsic commitment to the school is low, the ability of the social climate to elicit involvement is vital if order is to prevail. This inverse relationship is seen many times in any analysis of the human ecology of school crime.

In addition, a personalized social climate can significantly affect the attitudinal response of students to staff demands by offering the "compensation" of individuation and flexibility. Demands that may be acceptable in a small context because of its intimacy may be viewed as oppressive and authoritarian in the depersonalized large setting.[60] Schools rely on morale for their effective operation. It appears, however, that student morale has been on the decline, probably in some measure because of the trend toward large schools. This trend parallels the spread of academic disorder.

In this respect, the schools mirror the rest of society and are part of the larger problem of alienation. Alienation in U.S. society derives from the isolation of ages, individuals, and institutions from each other. The isolation of school from community is particularly severe.[61] Bronfenbrenner concludes that

> *As a result, the schools have become one of the most potent breeding grounds of alienation in American society. . . .*
>
> Above all, we must reverse the present trend toward the construction and administration of schools as isolated compounds divorced from the rest of the community.[62]

There can be no *genuine* freedom in schools unless there is a climate of order and security.[63] There is no genuine freedom in a prison or on a battlefield, and the problem of school crime threatens to turn schools into a combination of the two. To understand and solve the problem we must focus on the second-order effects that allow victim-perpetrator relationships to arise and persist. The foregoing discussion reveals that the social structure of the school can play a significant role (as a second-order effect) in the interpersonal behavior of students and staff. What remains is to translate this analysis into a series of guidelines for preventive and remedial action to inhibit school crime by strengthening the social fabric of U.S. schools.

From Understanding to Intervention

Three key policy questions are important here.

1. How can we organize schools to maximize social control, particularly where marginal students are concerned?
2. How can we generate and sustain a social climate in schools that motivates students to perform prosocial behaviors, and, in so doing, use the prosocial majority to control antisocial subgroups?
3. How can schools be protected from victimization by persons not part of the schools themselves?

The answer to all three questions lies in the enhancement of the role of the school as a potent, prosocial support system. We must make schools more effective in providing personal observation and feedback, in contingently reinforcing behavior, and in providing genuine opportunities for significant participation. Only by paying systematic attention to the social climate produced by school structure, size, and goals can we regulate behavior in student–student, teacher–student and victim–perpetrator relationships. To find an alternative to schools in which crime goes unchecked, we must make some changes in our thinking about what is important in a school. The following four goals state these needed changes. Together they outline a strategy for combating school crime that promises a humane alternative to schools "out of control," yet does not establish a police state within the classroom.

1. Create situational demands for participation. This is important if students are to develop a sense of responsibility for what goes on in the school. As we have learned from the problem of crime in general, law enforcement can be effective only when it has the support of the local citizenry. The application to school crime is clear: Reinforce responsibility in the student as "citizen." This is particularly important for the marginal student, whose academic citizenship is always in question.

2. Create a social climate in which *personal* observation, accountability, and feedback flourish. There is no substitute for the "cop on the beat" in the community at large. Likewise, there is no substitute for enduring, personalized relationships between staff and students.[64] Most teachers recognize that the foundation for basic social control is knowing the names of students. "George!" is infinitely superior to "Hey you!" Schools must operate as support systems.[65]

3. Strive for heterogeneity. Heterogenous settings encourage individualization and individuation. Individual responsibility is a key element in establishing a climate inhospitable to school crime. Moreover, heterogeneity permits the use of peer groups for prosocial ends where the social balance favors prosocial attitudes and behaviors.[66]

4. Arrange the contingencies to reinforce positively social competence and prosocial behavior. Where are the rewards in the school as a social system? Are they for individual success or for collective success? Are they for keeping one's nose clean or for being one's brother's keeper? Is good citizenship positively rewarded?

These four goals imply a systematic assessment of the school as a social system. Moreover, they imply the need for small schools. Small schools make the attainment of these goals feasible, even given the immense problems students bring with them to school. Two complementary forces dominate the human ecology of school crime: depersonalization of schools themselves through excessive size, and a general pattern of inadequate social identity.[67] The school can do little directly to combat the problem of alienation, although it can cooperate with other agencies. What the school can do, however, is to attend to issues of size and structure that can return a significant measure of control to prosocial forces. Small schools, emphasizing the creation and maintenance of enduring personalized social networks enmeshing students and staff, can be a great factor in the prevention and control of school crime. They can make an important contribution to successful schools and competent citizens.

Notes

1. G. Gallup, "12th Annual Gallup Poll of the Public's Attitude Toward the Public Schools," *Phi Delta Kappan* 62 (1980):33–46.

2. J. Wilson, "Crime in Society and Schools," *Educational Research* 5 (1976):3–6.

3. For example, F. Kanfer and A. Goldstein, *Helping People Change* (New York: Pergamon Press, 1975); J. Krumboltz and C. Thoresen, *Counseling Methods* (New York: Holt, Rinehart and Winston, 1976).

4. J. Garbarino, "The Human Ecology of Child Maltreatment," *Journal of Marriage and the Family* 39 (1977):721–736.

5. J. Rotter and D. Hochreich, *Personality* (New York: Scott-Foresman, 1975).

6. Kanfer and Goldstein, *Helping People Change;* Krumboltz and Thoresen, *Counseling Methods.*

7. Children's Defense Fund, *Children Out of School in America* (Washington, D.C.: Children's Defense Fund, 1974).

8. Garbarino, "The Human Ecology of Child Maltreatment."

9. J. McPartland and E. McDill, *The Unique Role of Schools in the Causes of Youthful Crime* (Baltimore, Md.: Johns Hopkins University, 1976); E. Wenk, *Schools and Delinquency Prevention* (Davis, Calif.: National Council on Crime and Delinquency, 1970).

10. R. Moos, "Evaluating and Changing Community Settings," *American Journal of Community Psychology* 4 (1976):313–326.

11. J. Garbarino, "The Meaning and Implications of School Success," *Educational Forum* 40 (1975):157–168.

12. Wenk, *Schools and Delinquency Prevention.*

13. U. Bronfenbrenner and M. Mahoney, "The Structure and Verification of Hypotheses," in *Influences on Human Development,* ed. U. Bronfenbrenner and M. Mahoney (Hinsdale, Ill.: Dryden Press, 1975); Garbarino, "The Human Ecology of Child Maltreatment."

14. G. Caplan and M. Killiea, *Support Systems and Mutual Help* (New York: Grune and Stratton, 1976); G. Caplan, *Support Systems and Community Mental Health* (New York: Behavioral Publications, 1974).

15. Caplan, *Support Systems and Community Mental Health,* pp. 4–5.

16. Ibid.

17. McPartland and McDill, *The Unique Role of Schools in Crime.*

18. K. Plath, *Schools Within Schools: A Study of High School Organization* (New York: Bureau of Publications, Teachers College, Columbia University, 1965).

19. For example, G. Barker and V. Gump, *Big School, Small School: High School Size and Student Behavior* (Stanford, Calif.: Standard University Press, 1964); L. Baird, "Big School, Small School: A Critical Examination of the Hypothesis," *Journal of Educational Psychology* 60 (1969):253–260; A. Wicker, "Cognitive Complexity, School Size and Participation in School Behavior Settings: A Test of the Frequency of Interaction Hypothesis," *Journal of Educational Psychology* 60 (1969):200–203.

20. J. Coleman, *The Adolescent Society* (New York: Free Press, 1961).

21. R. Dreeben, *On What Is Learned in School* (Reading, Mass.: Addison-Wesley, 1968).

22. Ibid, pp. 72–73.

23. J. Getzels, "Socialization and Education: A Note on Discontinuities," *Teachers College Record* 76(1974):218–225.

24. Ibid.

25. M. Burns, "The Case for Small Schools" (Speech before the Minnesota Interim Council on Education, Minneapolis, April 1968).

26. Barker and Gump, *Big School, Small School.*

27. J. Garbarino, "High School Size and Adolescent Social Development," *Human Ecology Forum* 4 (1973):26–29; J. Garbarino, "Some Thoughts on School Size and Its Effects on Adolescent Development," *Journal of Youth and Adolescence* 9 (1980):19–31.

28. J. Garbarino, "The Role of Schools in Socialization to Adulthood," *Educational Forum* 42 (1978):169–182.

29. Barker and Gump, *Big School, Small School.*

30. Ibid.

31. Ibid.

32. E. Willems, "Sense of Obligation to High School Activities as Related to School Size and Marginality of Student," *Child Development* 38 (1967):1247–1260.

33. For example, M. Grabe, "Big School, Small School: Impact of the High School Environment" (Paper presented at the Annual meeting of the American Educational Research Association, Washington, D.C., March 1975).

34. Baird, "Big School, Small School."

35. A. Wicker, "School Size and Students' Experiences in Extracurricular Activities: Some Possible Implications for School Planning," *Educational Technology* 9 (1969):44–47; J. Kleinert, "Effects of High School Size on Student Activity Participation," *NASSP Bulletin* 53 (1969):34–46.

36. C. Turner and M. Thrasher, *School Size Does Make a Difference* (San Diego, Calif.: San Diego Institute for Educational Management, 1970).

37. N. Rosenberg, "School Sizes as a Factor in School Expenditure, *Journal of Secondary Education* 45 (1970):135–142.

38. J. Burkhead, *Input and Output in Large-City Schools* (Syracuse, N.Y.: Syracuse University Press, 1967); J. Coleman et al., *Equality of Educational Opportunity* (Washington, D.C.: U.S. Government Printing Office, 1966).

39. U. Bronfenbrenner, "The Origins of Alienation," in *Influences on Human Development,* ed. Bronfenbrenner and Mahoney.

40. D. Blyth, R. Simmons, and D. Bush, "The Transition into Early Adolescence: A Longitudinal Comparison of Children in Two Educational Contexts" (Paper presented at the Biennial Meeting of the Society for Research in Child Development, New Orleans, La., 17–20 March 1977).

41. Barker and Gump, *Big School, Small School.*

42. Ibid., p. 198.

43. R. Barker and P. Schoggen, *Qualities of Community Life* (San Francisco: Jossey-Bass, 1973); Barker and Gump, *Big School, Small School.*

44. J. Conant, *The American High School Today: A First Report to Interested Citizens* (New York: McGraw-Hill, 1959); J. Jackson, *School Size and Program Quality in Southern High Schools* (Nashville, Tenn.: Center for Southern Educational Studies, George Peabody College for Teachers, 1966).

45. D. Heath, "Student Alienation and School," *School Review* 78 (1970):515–528.

46. E. Schumacher, *Small Is Beautiful: Economics As If People Mattered* (New York: Harper and Row, 1973).

47. B. Clark, in *Youth: Transition to Adulthood,* J. Coleman et al. (Chicago: University of Chicago Press, 1974), p. 79.

48. Ibid.

49. H. Averch et al., *How Effective is Schooling? A Critical Review of Research* (Englewood Cliffs, N.J.: Educational Technology Publications, 1974), p. 105.

50. Ibid.

51. Ford Foundation Report, *A Foundation Goes to School* (New York: Ford Foundation, 1972).

52. E. Wynne, "Privacy and Socialization to Adulthood" (Paper presented at the Annual Meeting of the American Educational Research Association, Washington, D.C., 31 March 1975).

53. Wilson, "Crime in Society and Schools."

54. Moos, "Evaluating and Changing Community Settings."

55. C. Buxton, *Adolescents in School* (New Haven, Conn.: Yale University Press, 1973).

56. Ibid.

57. Blyth, Simmons, and Bush, "The Transition into Early Adolescence."

58. New York State Temporary Commission to Study the Causes of Campus Unrest, "The Academy in Turmoil: First Report" (Albany, 1970); "Anarchy in the Academy: Second Report" (Albany, 1971); "Academy or Battleground: Third Report" (Albany, 1972).

59. New York State Temporary Commission, "The Academy in Turmoil," p. 59.

60. Schumacher, *Small Is Beautiful.*

61. Bronfenbrenner, "Origins of Alienation."

62. Ibid., p. 672.

63. M. Wolfgang, "Freedom and Violence," *Educational Researcher* 5 (1976):7–11.

64. Moos, "Evaluating and Changing Community Settings."

65. Caplan, *Support Systems and Community Mental Health;* Caplan and Killiea, *Support Systems and Mutual Help.*

66. R. Feldman, *The St. Louis Experiment: Group Interaction and Behavioral Change,* National Institute of Mental Health, Center for Studies of Crime and Delinquency Research Report Series (Washington, D.C.: U.S. Government Printing Office, 1974).

67. Garbarino, "Some Thoughts on School Size;" Bronfenbrenner, "Origins of Alienation."

7

Education beyond the High School

This chapter deals with the final stage of school success. Although there is and should be a social commitment to universal success at the secondary-school level, postsecondary education is another story. Success in the postsecondary institutions is surely important. There can be little doubt that a modern society requires that at least a small cadre of people attend school beyond the secondary level. Likewise, for those suited to it, postsecondary education can provide a variety of intellectually, interpersonally, and economically enriching experiences.

This discussion begins with a set of widely held assumptions about postsecondary education and its impact on the course of an individual's development. Recognizing these assumptions with respect to the consequences of postsecondary education should assist us in discussing its meaning and consequences.

A college education provides important economically relevant credentials.

A college education provides the highest development of the "academic culture" and, therefore, offers the greatest access to ·intellectual resources—art, music, literature, science, and all the other cultural accoutrements that promise to enrich the quality of life.

A college education enhances social status, both directly and indirectly.

A college education affects ideology in ways that influence major life decisions involving marriage, family size, childrearing style, response to authority, moral reasoning, and use of language.

A college education provides a context in which upwardly mobile, achievement-oriented youth and adults can have access to persons already part of elite groups, for the purpose of socialization and fraternization, thus enhancing overall social integration and cohesion.

In this view, postsecondary education is the *sine qua non* of the "good life" in all its many facets. Do postsecondary schools deliver the "goods" they promise? A better question might be, Who gets these goods, and who wants them? This discussion starts with the issue of American ambivalence about elite academics. Although public-opinion polls show a reservoir of support, there is a current of anti-intellectualism that endures and that was well expressed by a character in Willa Cather's 1922 novel *One of Ours*. When told that a local boy was "going abroad to study this Fall. He intends to be a professor", the character replies, "What's the matter with him? Does he have poor health."[1] We should not forget that sentiment.

Who Goes to College?

Until relatively recently, only a small proportion of the population attended college. This is still the case in most societies. In the United States, however, the percentage of 18-year-olds enrolling in some sort of college has climbed in the last four decades, from 19 percent in 1947 to 45 percent in 1977. The proportion of graduating high-school seniors going on to college has increased from 51 percent in 1954 to 59 percent in 1977.[2]

Faure and his colleagues reported the rates of attendance (percentage of 20- to 24-year-olds attending college) for the various regions of the world in 1967-1968.[3] These rates varied from 1.3 percent for Africa to 44.5 percent for North America. Europe and the USSR stood at 16.7 percent and Asia at 4.7 percent.[4] These figures indicate that the experience of college is substantially more widespread in the United States than anywhere else (or than it ever before has been in our own history). According to the Organization for Economic Co-operation and Development (OECD), the United States leads all other countries by a factor of at least 4 to 1 in the proportion of the population attending college.[5]

Current projections from a variety of sources indicate that the proportion entering U.S. colleges and universities will remain at about the same level (43 percent) for the indefinite future.[6] Although they indicate substantial change during the 1950s and 1960s, these figures do not do justice to the absolute magnitude of the changes—particularly during the 1960s, when the numbers of youth (aged 12 to 24) increased markedly (an increase of 52 percent from 1960 to 1970), and when the proportion of the total population they represented increased dramatically—39 percent during the period 1960-1970.[7] Thus, college education became a substantially larger social phenomenon during the 1950s and 1960s and is now a major fact of life for the workings of U.S. society. It places a far greater proportion of the population in a particular kind of institutional setting (with its concomitant ideology) than has ever been the case in any social system. From 1963 to 1973 the number of postsecondary students increased 86 percent, and the number of high-school graduates increased 35 percent.[8] These gross figures hide the fact that some colleges are "more equal" than others. Whereas there is relatively little differentiation among U.S. secondary schools (compared with British or European standards), there is a great deal of differentiation among our postsecondary institutions.

This differentiation exists along two dimensions. The horizontal dimension reflects the four major types of institutions: universities (four-year degree), colleges (four-year degree), junior colleges (two-year degree), and technical/vocational colleges (two-year degree). The vertical dimension locates institutions in terms of their prestige and relative academic quality. These distinctions make for a highly differentiated system.[9] There is some evidence to document the long-term impact of this pattern of differentiation.[10] However, the primary social impact of interest contained in the tripartite distinction is among those who complete a four-year degree (and, increasingly, some postgraduate degree); those who complete a two-year degree; and those who complete no degree at all.

Postsecondary-school attendance involves a substantial investment both by the individual and by the society (since even private tuition rarely covers more than one-third of the cost). On whose behalf is this investment made? McClelland noted that social class is more important than academic performance in influencing initial enrollment.[11] A higher proportion of students from affluent homes who have poor records enroll in college than of students with good academic records who come from less affluent families. After initial enrollment and after the first major selection process, academic ability and performance become more important as factors influencing completion. Sex also influences who is in college. Alexander's and Eckland's research shows that gender has an independent effect upon the likelihood of college attendance: females attend less often and are less likely to finish, regardless of social class.[12] That is, the investment is less likely to be made for females than males. We know that of those students who participated in postsecondary education (in 1978), 64 percent were in four-year institutions, whereas 36 percent attended two-year colleges ("community" or "junior" colleges). The National Center for Educational Statistics (NCES) projects that we will see a leveling off of this trend, with the figures stabilizing at 60-40 (four-year-two-year institutions) in the 1980s.[13] Second, there is a worldwide pattern favoring the enrollment in higher education of the children of those engaged in the "professions and management" over the children of "workers." Faure and his colleagues documented this difference but noted also that it is greater in some societies than in others.[14] Thus, for example, the ratio of college attendance to proportion of a particular group in the population is 6.07 for professions and management, and 0.20 for workers in Japan. It is 2.93 for professions and management, and 0.38 for workers in the United Kingdom. For the United States, the figures were 2.29 and 0.97, respectively.[15]

The data suggest that college attendance rates in the United States are less influenced by class differences than in most of the other societies, since the ratio of percentage of the college population to percentage of the total population for the two classes is most nearly equal. Only Yugoslavia, a collectivist socialist state, approximates the United States in this regard. Only in the United States does the working class have nearly its "share" of the college students. Even here, however, many more of the children of workers attend low-status two- and four-year institutions that do not lead to high-prestige outcomes.[16] This international comparison suggests that the investment in postsecondary education is a political matter of some importance. We can see this more clearly by examining a series of political issues surrounding the support systems for higher education in the United States and elsewhere.

The first area of interest is the provision of supports for continued attendance. These supports are needed to remove the economic costs to students who would otherwise be unable to attend for lack of funds. This applies particularly to postsecondary education, of course. As was noted before, the prospect of a student continuing education beyond high school is substantially greater if the family is affluent than if it is struggling or poor. Action of the political system can have and has had an important effect by providing the resources to allow the ideology of equality of opportunity to operate. Three examples of this kind of action may suffice.

The first concerns the role of publicly versus privately financed schooling. Obviously, in the economy of the educational marketplace the mixture of public and private institutions is a manifestation and a result of political policy. The City University of New York was a tuition-free institutional system that provided publicly supported access to schooling for millions of students. State universities are another example. In the case of the State University of New York, a deliberate, politically based policy of expansion to meet the rising tide of educational expectations in the post-World War II era resulted in dramatic change in the private-public "mix." Whereas in the early 1960s only one-third of the students in the state attended public institutions, by the 1970s more than two-thirds did so. Clearly, this is a function of political policy. The proportion of college students enrolled in publicly financed institutions rose from 55 percent nationwide in 1955 to 79 percent in 1980. It is expected to remain at this level at least until 1985.[17]

A second example involves government action to provide direct support to students (as opposed to indirect support through subsidizing institutions). The power of such support seems limited, however, as are, apparently, most programs aimed at individuals rather than groups or institutions. In an analysis of the impact of the GI Educational Benefits Program following World War II, Fogler and Nam found that despite the provision of quite substantial support, the GI bill resulted directly in "only" a 10-percent increase in attendance compared with the number who would have attended without it.[18] To be sure, it made the way substantially easier; but, easier or not, it appears that most of those who attended college would have done so anyway.

Based on the limited evidence available about the percent of veterans who would not have been able to continue their education without the GI Bill, it appears that a substantial majority would have continued their education, anyway, without any educational benefits.[19]

A final example comes from the Soviet Union. Halevy and Etzioni-Halevy compared the educational success of ethnic and racial groups in the Soviet Union in 1927 with that in 1970.[20] A strict government policy designed to redress group differences in university attendance caused some substantial changes to occur. These changes can be shown by comparing the ratio of university students from each ethnic group with that group's place in the total population. An index of 100 means a group has directly proportional representation in the university population. An index in excess of 100 indicates a greater than proportional representation. Some groups dramatically increased their index (for example, from 7 to 95 for Kazakhs), whereas others dramatically decreased theirs (for example, from 856 to 278 for Jews), whereas still others remained nearly the same (for example, from 106 to 112 for Russians). The rates of attendance (per 10,000 population) show both an overall increase and a trend toward equalization, from rates between 0.3 and 60 per 10,000 in 1927 to between 207 and 423 per 10,000 in 1970.[21] All these dramatic changes are, of course, the massive, "easy" ones—the changes from an underdeveloped to a modern society. As noted before, once a society achieves modernity, it becomes very difficult to manipulate school success directly.

Many studies have examined the etiology of college attendance.[22] Sewell and Shah considered the general relationship of ability and socioeconomic background to college attendance.[23] These data show that there is a substantial difference in the rate of college attendance as a function of social class, ability, and gender. The most likely to enroll are smart upper-class males (90.7); the least likely are less-able, poor females (3.7 percent). In later work Sewell outlines the role of socioeconomic status (SES) in more detail.[24] He presents the data in another manner, citing the odds in favor of children from higher socioeconomic backgrounds. For example, a high-SES student has 2.5 times as much chance as a low-SES student (of the same ability) of going on to post-high-school education of some kind. He has a 4-to-1 advantage in access to college, a 6-to-1 advantage in terms of college graduation, and a 9-to-1 advantage in likelihood of going on to graduate or professional education. If ability is held constant, low-SES persons are less likely to go on to college immediately after high school, are much less likely to attend or be graduated from high-quality colleges, are more likely to drop out if they enter college, and are less likely to return if they drop out.[25]

The sources of power in U.S. society are clearly reflected here. Moreover, these figures do not address the fact that these same factors influence the type (prestige and selectiveness) of institution attended. Solmon and Wachtel found that there are empirically demonstrable differences in the impact of different types of colleges (again in terms of prestige and selectiveness) on the economic and by implication the social lives of graduates.[26] Later work by Sewell and others also supports the influence of an individual's background on postsecondary schooling.[27] These differences (like the "quality" differences of high schools reported by both Coleman and Jencks) are associated with the background characteristics of the students. Wolfe did an analysis similar to Sewell and Shah's, but for the students in the 1950s, using not IQ but rank in high-school graduating class.[28] These data directly parallel Sewell and Shah's for a sample of students in the 1960s. Karabel also notes differences between colleges and describes what he sees as a "submerged class conflict within American higher education."[29] That is, community colleges occupy a lower position in the collegiate hierarchy mainly because of their liberal admission policies and the supposedly corresponding lower ability level of their students (many more of whom come from low-SES backgrounds as compared with students at four-year institutions). Data for the 1970s are consistent with those for the previous decades on the matter of social class, but showed virtually no sex difference (65 percent versus 64 percent for affluent males and females, versus 40 percent for poor males and females).[30]

Perhaps the most-sophisticated study of this phenomenon was conducted by Christensen, Melder, and Weisbrod.[31] They identified the relative importance of ability, class, and sex in influencing college attendance for a sample of Wisconsin students in the 1960s. Their results give the probability of attending college as a function of *combinations* of class, ability, and sex. Overall, the probability of attending college is far greater for average males (0.44) than for average females (0.23)—except when there is a local college, where females (0.59) are more likely to attend than males (0.44). The other factors studied (such as parents' income and education) all have effects that are greater for females than for males.[32] Thus, for example, males with mothers who have eight years of schooling or less are much more likely to attend than are comparable females (0.44 versus 1.07).[33]

In the 1970s, postsecondary-school success took the place that high-school graduation held in the 1930s and 1940s. Its function as a socio-economic credential is in many ways similar, since it is the prerequisite for the white-collar occupations. Therefore, we may expect that the dynamics of dropping out of college in the 1970s will resemble those of dropping out of high school in the 1930s and 1940s and will be different from those of dropping out of high school in the 1960s and the 1970s. This appears to be the case.

Sewell and Shah's analysis again provides some detailed data that address the factors influencing whether or not one completes college.[34] They reported that the likelihood of graduating from college parallels the likelihood of enrolling in the first place: sex, social class, and IQ all play an important role—for example, 6.7 percent of the low-ability, poor females finish, as opposed to 70.6 percent of the high-ability, affluent males.

They conclude that:

> Whereas males are more influenced by intelligence than by socioeconomic origins and females are more influenced by socioeconomic origins than by intelligence throughout the process of selection in higher education, both factors continue to operate on both sexes.[35]

Data for the 1970s support these conclusions.[36] They show similar dropout rates for college students of different class backgrounds, ability, and sex. Whereas 41 percent of the low-ability students who started college in 1972 dropped out by 1973, only 14 percent of the high-ability students (and 28 percent of the average-ability students) had done so. In each category the rates were higher for girls and for the nonaffluent. A major source of the sex differences in these data and in comparable data for high schools is the impact of the role of parenthood for females. Pregnancy and marriage are the two most-significant (and, of course, related) causes of the higher dropout rate for females than for males.

There is, however, another kind of college experience that is important to our discussion, that of students who return to college after leaving, as well as the broader phenomenon of adult attendance at college. According to the NCES, 29 percent of those enrolled in 1972 were over 24 years old; by 1978 the figure had risen to 35 percent.[37] Total college-enrollment figures for those less than 24 years old climbed only slowly from 1972 (peaking at 15 percent above the 1972 figure in 1976), whereas the enrollment of older students climbed at a much faster rate (up 62 percent from the 1972 figure in the peak year of 1977). More than 50 percent of the increased enrollment in two-year colleges and more than 33 percent of the rise in undergraduate enrollment in four-year colleges and universities was due to the presence of older students.[38]

Who are these adult students? The experience of one college that specializes in such adult students indicates that some 80 percent of them have previously been students at some institution of higher learning.[39] This may provide a partial answer to the questions posed by dropouts. They tend to reenroll after dropping out, and many ultimately complete degrees. We also know that older students differ from their younger colleagues in a number of ways in addition to age. First and foremost, they are not primarily students; that is, the classroom is not the main focus of their lives. Many older students have been (and may continue to be) business people, technicians, homemakers, or engaged in a variety of other occupations. Also, many are married and have families of their own. Therefore, student experiences constitute only one segment of their lives.[40] Second, they have different concerns regarding schooling than do many younger students. For example, many more report feeling unprepared for college as compared with traditional students (33 percent as opposed to 92 percent, in 1978).[41] They also report concern about the price of education, the availability of special programs, and residency requirements (regulations requiring that a certain number of credit hours toward a degree must be completed on campus).[42] A third difference between older and younger students is attendance status. Many older students attend classes only part time. The enrollment of part-time learners in colleges and universities nearly doubled between 1968 and 1978, mainly because of the influx of older "part timers." The U.S. Bureau of the Census reports that two out of three older students attend college part time, whereas only one out of ten "traditionally" aged students do so.[43] Part-time enrollment is also a general trend that colleges will have to face. The NCES revealed that part-time students now make up over 30 percent of all undergraduate enrollment and about 60 percent of the graduate totals.[44] A final point regarding part-time older students is that the majority of them attend two-year colleges.

What does all this mean for colleges? It certainly demands that institutions of higher learning modify existing practices. It may mean a redefinition of education as well. Many colleges and universities have already begun to change their policies to meet the needs of the older student. For example, many colleges offer external degree programs that allow students to complete part or all of a degree without coming to the "main campus." Also, some institutions are beginning to broaden their view of what constitutes a valid educational experience to include volunteer work or professional experiences of various kinds. In essence, they are acknowledging that a college education is more than a certain number of pages written or books read.[45] What do we know of the effects of reentry on the adults themselves, on their family and marriage roles, ideology and behavior, vocational and cognitive development? What little we do know indicates that the problems are substantial and the payoffs for meeting them great.

It seems reasonable to anticipate significant changes in colleges and in the socialization experiences they represent as a result of this growing pattern. We may consider this change in light of the characteristic demographic profile of U.S. colleges. They have clearly been a kind of youth ghetto, places where individuals of a narrowly circumscribed age range (that of youth) live together in a situation of heightened intensity. What are the effects of participating in such a youth ghetto? Has the marked increase in number of adult students mediated these effects in any way? We do not know very much about these issues. Our real concern is with this question: How has the change in college-attendance patterns affected the role of postsecondary-school success in shaping the individual and collective lives of Americans?

The Social Impact of Postsecondary Schooling

When we consider colleges as contexts for socialization, we find that most of our conclusions about high schools still apply. Largeness decreases participation and identity, and alienation is a significant problem. As McClelland points out, relative achievement in college is of little importance to life outcomes when compared with the dichotomy of passing and graduating versus failing and dropping out.[46] The vertical differences among colleges, although important, are less significant than the dichotomy between attending and not attending, when it comes to the effects produced by the experience of a postsecondary education.[47]

The discontinuity experienced by college students from other than middle-class, affluent backgrounds appears to be a function of the socioeconomic climate presented by the college itself. This was brought out by two studies.[48] Ellis and Lane examined the experience of students from "lower-status backgrounds" in the context of a private, upper-middle-status, residential university. They found that in such a setting these students, although performing well in the academic and athletic realms (an artifact due perhaps to their admission as high-achieving scholarship students) were "judged to be unpopular, reported fewer dates, and were less likely to join a fraternity."[49] Wegner's study presents a contrasting picture. He studied students at a public university where most students live at home and commute to school and in which all social classes are represented in great numbers. He found that there was no evidence of social or psychological maladjustment as a function of class background. Wegner's conclusion summarizes the point of this contrast:

> . . . environment and other contextual effects of the college may be critical for mobile students. Which college a lower class student attends may have a great deal of influence on whether he will experience psychological problems there.[50]

These results parallel those of another study by Wegner, in which he found that "lower-status students were found to be more successful in completing work for their degrees if they attended state colleges than if they went to private liberal arts colleges or a prestigious university."[51] "Manners" (in the broadest sense of the term) are learned by students who have ability coupled with a strong motivation for upward mobility. Jencks concluded that the combination of "credentials" and "style" is the chief outcome of college, the one with the greatest social consequences.[52] How has the change from dominance of the college "market" by private, elite colleges to dominance by "mass," state-supported institutions affected the social meaning of college? How has college changed as the source of elite culture, upper-middle-class manners, and potent credentials?

Turner undertook an analysis of the concepts of "sponsored" versus "contest" social mobility.[53] In cases of sponsored mobility, the elite (and their agents) select those destined for upward mobility. In contest mobility, mobility is a prize taken in an open contest by the efforts of the individual. These two contrasting systems, as reflected in the British and U.S. approaches to postsecondary education, cast school and schooling in different lights.

> In sponsored mobility, the main purpose of education is to promote elite culture, and those forms of education which do so are more highly valued than those that do not. Schooling of the non-elite is hard to justify and is usually low on the list of educational priorities, while the "maximum educational resources are concentrated on 'those who can benefit most from them'." Within the paradigm of contest mobility, however, education is the means of getting ahead, but is not valued in its own right.[54]

This affects the role of colleges as transmitters of "high" culture. Another consequence is the difference in "victory" rates once college is begun. In England more than 80 percent of the students who initially enroll complete degrees, as opposed to about 50 percent in the United States.

These differences complement other differences in the role and nature of elites. Britain has been much more dependent on a small cadre of elite public servants, all of whom shared nearly identical socialization experiences by being "at school" together (principally at Oxford and Cambridge). There is only a glimmer of this in the United States—the Ivy League, on the one hand, and the regional schools linked to local political power and opportunity on the other. The United States is too big and too much based on contest mobility for the British system to work well. (Recent events suggest that Britain itself may no longer be able to make such a system work well.) In addition, the concept of a shared "classical" education in the liberal arts declines as the consensus on what constitutes a quality education breaks down.

The Processes and Ideology of
Postsecondary Schooling

Daniel Yankelovich's polls of the ideology of college students reveal interesting patterns, which illuminate the relationships between higher education as a system and other components of the human ecology.[55] Of particular interest are the changes reported in the relative position of two contrasting ideologies, "traditional-vocational" versus "modern-humanistic." Yankelovich reports that as the socioeconomic impact of college has eroded (that is, as a "good" job after graduation has become less of a guarantee), the traditional-vocational ideology has come into ascendence. He reports an increase in those college students who see college as "career training" (in contrast to a vehicle for self-discovery and change) from 55 percent in 1968 to 66 percent in 1973.[56] A recent study projects that in excess of 1 million college graduates will go jobless in the 1980s.[57] As a response, some college students have apparently shifted their concern away from the enlightening aspects of a college education toward its "training" aspects. This is the case according to a survey of twenty student-body presidents from large universities (15,000 or more student population) conducted in the spring of 1979.[58] Fourteen of the presidents said that business would rank first among students' choice of profession in their schools. (This is in line with the report by half the universities involved in the survey that enrollment in their schools of business was up 50 percent in the last five years.) According to the presidents, student concerns today are radically different from those of ten years ago. Seventeen out of twenty see the state of the economy as the most pressing problem facing the United States today. It seems that "students no longer feel a great urgency to create a new order. They are more concerned with their own lives."[59] Data from the American Council of Education's annual survey of college freshmen provides a good summary of the shift in attitudes among the collegiate population. Among other questions, the council asks freshmen to rate a list of objectives as important or unimportant in their lives. The results over the last ten years indicate that "being well off financially" was cited as important by 62 percent in 1979 (versus 19 percent in 1969), and that the importance of personal growth and civic responsibility had declined by nearly half.[60]

The 1960s were in many ways demographically and socioeconomically unique. A massive increase in the youth population paralleled an expanding economy. Moreover, the character of the economy was changing to encourage a large increase in nonindustrial, white-collar jobs. These forces made for a fertile soil in which colleges and the modern-humanistic ideology could flourish. The freedom of affluence permitted and encouraged a pattern of collegiate autonomy and security—both during and after schooling. As both demographic and economic conditions have changed, the dominant collegiate ideology has likewise changed. The 1970s marked a return to a more likely social pattern, the 1960s having been in many ways atypical. We have seen a leveling off of the proportion of high-school graduates enrolling in postsecondary education (at about 43 percent). This represents a substantial increase over the pre-1960s level (of approximately 30 percent). It seems that the current figure may become fixed.[61] Since we as a society have developed the taste for college and have established the necessary infrastructure, it seems unlikely that the figure will drop below the current level. On the other hand, it seems unlikely that we will expand our system of postsecondary education. There is no pressing demand for college graduates to fill white-collar jobs. As noted previously, most of the new jobs will be in industrial and service areas, requiring only a high-school diploma or at most a two-year vocational training program. Furthermore, there is no evidence of any great numbers of prospective students among the youth population. The trend toward continuing education should provide any increases that do occur. Adult students generally are already established in vocational roles and go back to school either to consolidate their position or to gain intellectual stimulation and enlightenment.

Another aspect of colleges in relation to the general operation of the human ecology is evident in the response of colleges to a decline in the basic skills of entering students. As was noted before, the Scholastic Aptitude Test (SAT) scores of U.S. youth have declined steadily since 1963 (when the zenith was reached after nearly two decades of increase). Most colleges report having to institute remedial and/or developmental programs in the area of basic scholastic skills (particularly writing). For example, a recent report indicates that fully one-third of the entering students in the Pennsylvania State University system fail to meet basic skill levels. Edward Hollander, the New Jersey chancellor of higher education, reported that 80 percent of the students in New Jersey colleges have had some form of remedial instruction and that half of the freshman being admitted will need some kind of special tutoring in order to keep from failing.[62] This problem is also reflected in the attitudes of students toward the quality of preparation for work or college they received in their high schools. NCES documented this in a longitudinal study of the high-school class of 1972.[63] This group was polled (in 1976) regarding the training and counseling they had received in high school. Less than 13 percent felt that their schools had provided counseling that helped them find work or continue their education. Our own experience with young people provides anecdotal evidence of this problem. A colleague reports that many of his former students feel that their high schools failed to prepare them either academically or socially for college; they wished for a program that placed more emphasis on basic skills and the development of self-discipline and a sense of responsibility.

However, given what we know about the difficulties of successful remediation where there is no underlying academic foundation, it seems unlikely that colleges will do much better. The teaching effectiveness of colleges will in all likelihood be shown to match that of high schools—in a word, minimal. Whatever is not there when the student arrives, the odds are that it will not be there when the student leaves the institution. This problem can only be remedied at an earlier point in the developmental process. Colleges seem to be effective only in providing resources that the active student can employ in self-directed development.

We can amplify this conclusion by looking at the process and criteria by which colleges select students for admission. It has been customary for colleges to deal with relatively narrow ranges of student ability. Within these narrow ranges they can establish relative criteria for achievement. The selection process leads to relatively homogeneous groupings and screens a number of phenomena that, when exposed, call into question the supposed "teaching effectiveness" of colleges. The selection process provides an excuse for the performance of students in some colleges and gives a false sense of efficacy to the teachers in other colleges. If a broad range of student abilities are present, this system breaks down and undermines the meaning of "college"-level performance. How can the excellent work of a student at a prestigious elite college be compared, let alone equated, with the excellent performance of a student at an institution with little status and an open-admissions policy?[64]

As Chickering and McCormick note, the typical pattern makes it easy to grade students and establish standards based on the "normal" student for a particular institution.[65] But if we put all these classes of students together in the same particular institution, the problem of "standards" becomes extremely difficult. This differentiation of institutions on the basis of student entrance characteristics is the U.S. equivalent of the British secondary system of "public" (private), grammar, and secondary-modern schools. Whereas the British carry out recruitment of elites at the secondary level, we leave it to the tertiary level. What difference do these differences make? The evidence suggests that these differences have their major impact on colleges as credentializing institutions. Completion of a degree at a low-status college as opposed to a high-status college, for example, has some impact on social and vocational opportunities.[66]

We have emphasized the structure and form of higher education, but it is also worth taking note of its process. Quality results from the establishment of a direct intellectual relationship with academically competent teachers. Wilson and Gaff demonstrated this in a study of "effective" college professors.[67] The results of their study are relevant to the present discussion. Effective college teachers (as identified by both students and colleagues) are characterized by commitment to undergraduate teaching, efforts to make presentations interesting through the use of relevant examples and analogies, and the extent to which they engage in serious discussions with students outside of class.[68] So much for academic process. It is reassuring to find that good teaching consists of good teaching in the classic sense. Put more directly, effective college teaching depends on serious intellectual interaction. Personalized, committed interaction is the *sine qua non* of collegiate education, as it seems to be at the elementary and secondary level as well. As in counseling and psychotherapy, ideology and gimmicks are less important than genuine, serious interaction. Other investigations support these results.[69] The intellectual process of postsecondary schooling is essentially one of modeling and social reinforcement. Competent teachers demonstrate the operational meaning of scholarship and encourage the students who are motivated to perform these behaviors.

The Outcomes of Postsecondary-School Success

Having examined some of the social and psychological foundations of postsecondary schooling, we can return to our initial concerns. First, we wished to know how postsecondary schooling related to earlier school success. It appears that in the United States in the 1980s, the college experience has in many ways become an important positive screening device. Whereas failure in the secondary schools is debilitating and in many ways socially unjust, "failure" at the postsecondary level is neither debilitating nor particularly unjust (although initial access to higher education is certainly somewhat inequitable). Life for the high-school graduate is likely to meet the requirement of social habitability, with generally adequate access to necessary social and economic resources. Unlike the high-school dropout, the college dropout is *not* a member of a deviant minority. Thus, postsecondary-school success serves a useful social function. It provides for a large elite (some 25 percent of the population) who have advanced credentials and academic experience. A modern society needs such an elite. The only major injustice remaining in the system is that although the affluent of low ability usually have access to college, the nonaffluent often do not. To answer our second concern, postsecondary education does meet the goals set for it in the minds of most Americans.

College does appear to provide credentials with important economic and social consequences. Lately, the economic impact has been sharply eroded as the gap between college and trade-school education has begun to disappear; but the role of college as a route of access to status, prestige, and a self-directed middle-class work setting and life-style continues to be crucial and promises to remain so.[70] This obtains despite the fact that 75 to 80 percent of the new job opportunities in the 1980s are in areas *requiring* only a high-school diploma.

College does seem to maximize the development of the academic culture, with the expected impact on the educational development of children. There is some question, however, about its effectiveness in enhancing the quality of life in subjective terms. For reasons cited by Jencks, there may not be *recognition* of a higher-quality existence because of the tendency of people to make comparisons *within* socioeconomic strata, not across them.[71] It seems clear that the "objective" impact on the quality of life is substantial and is revealed in virtually all studies that in some way assess quality of life.

Sonderstrom's research on religious orientation and the meaningfulness of life may be instructive here.[72] We ought to be distrubed by his finding that those whose orientation is "humanistic" (low religious orientation, high social commitment) are lowest on measures of meaningfulness. It appears that the consequence of the "rationalizing" processes inherent in U.S. colleges (with the possible exception of religiously oriented institutions) is exactly that "humanistic" orientation. The issue is not whether or not such an orientation can or should be enhanced by the experience of college. Rather, it is whether or not the widespread development of the humanistic orientation bodes well or ill for the habitability of the human ecology and the personal integration of each individual's identity. People seem to need a sense of transcendence—a spiritual as opposed to a materialist conception of the world and their place in it. The consequences of an elite system of higher education (in which the humanistic orientation is confined to a small group) may prove to have important differences from those of a system of mass higher education. There is little clear and direct evidence on this issue, however. A society can usefully employ a humanist, rational elite to provide special services to its institutional and cultural life but may be unable to sustain this orientation on a mass level except at the risk of unacceptably widespread alienation. Fortunately, as it were, the effect of mass higher education is probably relatively small.

The experience of college does provide enhanced social status by opening important doors and by training students in manners. This effect is dependent on the prestige of the college and on the student's ability and willingness to accept the socialization experiences it offers. A high level of academic competence can provide substantial opportunities for upward mobility. It leads to what the political philosopher Pareto called the "circulation of elites."[73] Both the ideology of the class system and the processes by which material support for higher education operate ensure the operation of these conditions. We are set up to recruit talented and willing youth into elites on the basis of their competence in the process of contest mobility.[74] This is reassuring if we can in fact provide equitable access into our system of higher education. As long as we do not get caught up in a futile and self-defeating campaign for universal postsecondary education, the nation's system of colleges and universities will be fine, even allowing for the enrollment declines of the 1980s. Declining enrollment may bring hard times to many institutions, but it may also help bring postsecondary schooling back into an appropriate perspective.

Notes

1. W. Cather, *One of Ours* (New York: A.A. Knopf, 1922).

2. National Center for Educational Statistics (NCES), U.S. Department of Education, *The Condition of Education* (Washington, D.C.: U.S. Government Printing Office, 1980).

3. E. Faure et al., *Learning to Be* (Paris: UNESCO, 1972).

4. Ibid.

5. Organization for Economic Co-operation and Development (OECD), *Education, Inequality, and Life Chances* (Paris: OECD, 1975).

6. NCES, *The Condition of Education,* 1980.

7. J. Coleman et al., *Youth: Transition to Adulthood* (Chicago: University of Chicago Press, 1974).

8. K. Simon and M. Frankel, NCES, U.S. Department of Education, *Projections of Educational Statistics to 1983-84* (Washington, D.C.: U.S. Government Printing Office, 1974).

9. J. Karabel, "Community Colleges and Social Stratification," *Harvard Educational Review* 42 (1972):521-562; J. Karabel, "Protecting the Portals: Class and the Community College," *Social Policy* 5 (1974):19-24.

10. L. Solmon and P. Wachtel, "The Effects on Income of Type of College Attended," *Sociology of Education* 48 (1975):75-90.

11. D. McClelland, "Testing for Competence Rather Than for Intelligence," *American Psychologist* 28 (1973):1-14.

12. K. Alexander and B. Eckland, "Contextual Effects in the High School Attainment Process," *American Sociological Review* 40 (1975):402-416.

13. NCES, *The Condition of Education.*

14. Faure, *Learning to Be.*

15. Ibid.

16. Karabel, "Community Colleges and Social Stratification;" Karabel, "Protecting the Portals."

17. NCES, *The Condition of Education,* 1980.

18. J. Folger and C. Nam, *Education of the American Population* (Washington, D.C.: U.S. Government Printing Office, 1967).

19. Ibid., p. 28.

20. Z. Halevy and E. Etzioni-Halevy, "The Religious Factor and Achievement in Education," *Comparative Education* 10 (1974):193-199.

21. Ibid.

22. W. Sewell and V. Shah, "Socioeconomic Status, Intelligence and the Attainment of Higher Education," *Sociology of Education* 40 (1967):1-23; NCES, *The Condition of Education;* D. Wolfe, "Educational Opportunity, Measured Intelligence and Social Background," in *Education, Economy and Society: A Reader in the Sociology of Education,* ed. A. Halsey,

J. Floud, and C. Anderson (New York: Free Press, 1961); N. Rogoff, "Local Structure and Educational Selection" in *Education, Economy and Society*, ed. Halsey, Floud, and Anderson; S. Christensen, J. Melder, and B. Weisbrod, "Factors Affecting College Attendance," *Journal of Human Resources* 10 (1975):176-188; K. Wilson and A. Portes, "The Educational Attainment Process: Results from a National Sample," *American Journal of Sociology* 81 (1975):343-361; J. Meyer, "High School Effects on College Intentions," *American Journal of Sociology* 76 (1970):59-69; A. Kerckhoff and J. Huff, "Parental Influence on Educational Goals," *Sociometry* 37 (1974):307-327.

23. Sewell and Shah, "Attainment of Higher Education."

24. W. Sewell, "Inequality of Opportunity for Higher Education," *American Sociological Review* 36 (1971):793-807.

25. Ibid.

26. Solmon and Wachtel, "The Effects on Income."

27. W. Sewell, "Social Mobility and Social Participation," *Annals of the American Academy of Political and Social Science* 435 (1978):226-247; O. Duncan, D. Featherman, and B. Duncan, *Socioeconomic Background and Achievement* (New York: Seminar Press, 1972); C. Jencks et al., *Who Gets Ahead?* (New York: Basic Books, 1979); R. de Leon, *Small Futures* (New York: Harcourt, Brace, Jovanovich, 1979); D. Featherman and R. Hauser, "Changes in the Socioeconomic Stratification of the Races," *American Journal of Sociology* 82 (1976):621-651.

28. Wolfe, "Educational Opportunity."

29. Karabel, "Community Colleges and Social Stratification."

30. NCES, Education Division, U.S. Department of Health, Education and Welfare, *The Condition of Education: A Statistical Report on the Condition of American Education* (Washington, D.C.: U.S. Government Printing Office, 1975).

31. Christensen, Melder, and Weisbrod, "Factors Affecting College Attendance."

32. Ibid.

33. Ibid.

34. Sewell and Shah, "Attainment of Higher Education."

35. Ibid., pp. 21-22.

36. NCES, *The Condition of Education,* 1975.

37. NCES, *The Condition of Education,* 1980.

38. R. Miller, "A Decade of Data on Adult Learners," *College Board Review* 114 (1979-1980):16-17.

39. W. Bradley, "Profiles of Empire State College Students" (Saratoga Springs, N.Y.: Empire State College, 1974).

40. S. Leckie, "The New Student on Campus," *Educational Horizons* 56 (1978):196-199.

41. Miller, "A Decade of Data."

42. Ibid.

43. Ibid.

44. Ibid.

45. Leckie, "The New Student on Campus."

46. McClelland, "Testing for Competence."

47. A. Chickering and J. McCormick, "Pesonality Development and the College Experience," *Research in Higher Education* 1 (1973):43-70.

48. R. Ellis and W. Lane, "Social Mobility and Social Isolation: A Test of Sorokin's Dissatisfaction Hypothesis," *American Sociological Review* 32 (1967):237-253; E. Wegner, "The Effects of Upward Mobility: A Study of Working-Status College Students," *Sociology of Education* 46 (1973):263-279.

49. Ellis and Lane, "Social Mobility and Social Isolation."

50. Wegner, "The Effects of Upward Mobility," p. 227.

51. E. Wegner and W. Sewell, "Selection and Context as Factors Affecting the Probability of Graduation from College," *American Journal of Sociology* 75 (1970):665-668.

52. C. Jencks, *Inequality: A Reassessment of the Effect of Family and Schooling in America* (New York: Basic Books, 1972).

53. R. Turner, "Modes of Social Ascent Through Education: Sponsored and Contest Mobility," in *Education, Economy and Society,* ed. Halsey, Floud, and Anderson.

54. Ibid., p. 130.

55. D. Yankelovich, Inc., *The Changing Values on Campus: Political and Personal Attitudes of Today's College Students* (New York: Washington Square Press, 1972).

56. D. Yankelovich, *The New Morality: A Profile of American Youth in the 70's* (New York: McGraw-Hill, 1974).

57. D. Hecker, "The Jam at the Bottom of the Funnel: The Outlook for College Graduates," *Occupational Outlook Quarterly* 22 (1978):36-39.

58. G. Budig, "Student Attitudes in 1979," *Educational Record* 60 (1979):301-304.

59. Ibid., p. 304.

60. J. Butler, "Portrait of an Era," *Educational Record* 61 (1980):73-75.

61. NCES, *The Condition of Education,* 1980.

62. NCES, U.S. Department of Education, *The American High School: A Statistical Review* (Washington, D.C.: U.S. Government Printing Office, 1980).

63. Ibid.

64. Chickering and McCormick, "Personality Development and the College Experience."

65. Ibid.

66. Solmon and Wachtel, "The Effects on Income."

67. R. Wilson and J. Gaff, *College Professors and Their Impact on Students* (New York: John Wiley and Sons, 1975).

68. Ibid.

69. For example, J. Garbarino and U. Bronfenbrenner, "Research on Parent-Child Relations and Social Policy: How to Proceed," Boys Town Center for the Study of Youth Development Working Paper, Series 1, 1977.

70. M. Kohn, *Class and Conformity: A Study in Values, with a Reassessment* (Chicago: University of Chicago Press, 1977).

71. Jencks, *Inequality.*

72. D. Soderstrom, "Religious Orientation and Meaning in Life," *Journal of Clinical Psychology* 33 (1977):65-68.

73. V. Pareto, *The Rise and Fall of the Elites* (Totowa, New Jersey: Bedminster Press, 1968).

74. R. Turner, "Modes of Social Ascent Through Education: Sponsored and Context Mobility," in *Education, Economy and Society,* ed. Halsey, Floud, and Anderson.

8 The Current Context of School Success

An Outline of the Origins and Processes of School Success

Our model of school success is a direct response to the standard U.S. educational-research paradigm. It substitutes a modified version of educational attainment for relative academic achievement as the definition of school success. According to our definition, to succeed in school one must develop the intellectual and social skills necessary to achieve promotion and preserve the opportunity for access to the next-higher level of schooling. Chapter 2 outlined the conceptual and empirical rationale for this position. Although relative academic achievement (grades and test scores) are context and time bound in their impact, our concept of school success is not. Given the mission and social function of schooling in the process of socialization from childhood through adolescence to adulthood, a valid definition of school success must involve its significant long-term influence on the course of development. We believe our definition has such ecological validity and integrity.

Our analysis of the origins of school success has taken a "radical" approach to the problem. We have attempted to look at the roots of the phenomenon. This has meant an examination of the forces throughout the social environment that shape the student's access to and competence in schools. Our main focus has been the interplay of political, economic, social, and psychological forces in encouraging and equipping some students while thwarting others. We have examined the importance of factors *within* the school as they are determined by the context established by factors *outside* the school, and have explored the ways in which the outcomes of schooling for an individual are the result of the very complex interaction of what the school is and what the student is. Forces emanating from the institutional and ideological systems shape both school and students. Having explicated this model, we can proceed to some specific social issues implicating school success. These issues are central to the social conditions of schooling that provide the interplay of schools and habitability.

School Success and Social Policy: What Are the Issues?

What are the major policy issues involving schools that currently face U.S. society? There are many, but we may usefully consider three. First, there is the general issue involved in using the schools as vehicles for social engineering. The current focal point for such efforts is the use of schools to reduce racial segregation. We need to know *how* to plan, implement, and assess such social engineering, particularly with respect to its effects on school success.

Second, there is the general problem of educational investment. Given our increasing recognition that resources are limited, how should they be invested in schooling? Is there a saturation point beyond which further investment produces diminishing returns? If cuts must be made, how can we minimize their impact on essential activities? How can we best invest monies designated for compensatory education and intervention programs? In all these issues, the meaning of school success is fundamental. All questions of educational investment must address school success, which should be and is one of the foundations of our model of education.

Third, there is the question of the school's role in maintaining a habitable social environment for children and youth. The social climate of schools and their impact on the processes of socialization is a major issue in U.S. society. The relative importance of academic and social development is the focal point here. Should the curriculum of the schools focus on teaching values and building character? Can prosocial development be fostered without serious cost to academic growth? The concept of school success we have developed in our discussion can illuminate these issues. Since this concept puts pure academic achievement in an ecologically valid perspective and focuses on the dominant role of social forces in producing success in school, it can show us how to balance academic achievement and social identity in a way that contributes optimally to the overall development of children and youth.

Social Engineering for Racial Justice

Certainly the most-serious and most-controversial issues surrounding educational policy stem from attempts to deal with the problem of racial segregation. After decades of blatant discrimination, the 1950s saw the first legal movement toward justice, followed by the first wave of real action in the 1960s. In the 1970s, court-ordered programs designed to override residential segregation through redistricting, racial-balance quotas, and redistribution of students through busing were dominant themes, which continue into the 1980s as major issues.[1] Public-opinion polls in the 1980s indicate overwhelming rejection of such busing (with 72 percent of whites and 56 percent of blacks indicating opposition, figures that have changed little since 1970).[2] In fact, very few U.S. residents support the movement of children to new schools in any manner as a means of integration.[3] No one who reads the newspapers needs to be told that desegration and integration make tremendous demands on the wisdom, strength, and courage of communities and their leaders.

Educational research in this area, like social-science research in general, has pursued a divided course with respect to the relationship of scientific knowledge to social policy. Some researchers have seen this mission as one of developing basic pure science and have therefore eschewed questions of social policy in their research (although not necessarily in their popular writing). Others have sought to study the implementation of educational policy and its impact on the academic and social behavior of students and teachers. These researchers have tried to develop an applied science of education. As Crain has noted, however, these two approaches have been at odds.[4] The pure scientists deny the value of applied or policy work, whereas those studying applied questions have generally been unable or unwilling to link their work to larger social or intellectual contexts. This problem of the proper relationship of research to social policy, and vice versa, has increasingly been recognized in the social sciences,[5] as well as in the natural sciences.[6] Nowhere is this more apparent than in the area of school desegregation. As Crain has pointed out, research on the effects of school desegregation has been disappointing and even dangerous.[7] After reviewing the evidence, he concluded that the design and interpretation of the studies has not aided in the difficult process of evaluation.

> In what way has social research helped the nation resolve the issue of school desegregation? The answer seems to be in no way.[8]

As desegregation efforts have proceeded, the confusion has grown rather than diminished. As both Crain and St. John have shown, the research results are ill equipped to provide the answers so desperately needed.[9] Ideologies, whether for or against desegregation efforts, have used the available evidence to promote their own interests.

At the heart of the problem is a lack of clarity about the goals of desegregation. The obvious starting point for a critique of racial segregation is that it is unjust, immoral, and unconstitutional. On these grounds alone it is subject to political action designed to eliminate it.[10] However, the issue has been defined more broadly. Our concern as a society has been directed to the developmental consequences of segregation and efforts at desegregation.

Research on the effects of desegregation has focused on two areas: academic achievement and social development. St. John reviewed the evidence in both these areas and found a confused and confusing picture emerging.[11] The studies of social development have focused on self-concept. Rarely, if ever, have studies looked at the long-term impact on socialization to adulthood. Most studies are only one year in duration, hardly enough time for a valid assessment of any genuinely significant impact on social development.[12]

The studies of academic achievement present similar problems. They also are usually of insufficient duration to permit any genuine change. More importantly, the almost exclusive emphasis on academic achievement is, according to our model, inappropriate. The dependent variable in these analyses should be school success. The gist of our analysis has been that school success (as opposed to, and unlike, simple academic achievement) is largely under the control of social forces. Desegregation is primarily a social event. It touches the key processes of social influence—modeling, reinforcement, attribution, and role taking—all of which are involved in the acquisition of the basic skills needed for school success. There is every reason to expect that, when it is competently handled, desegregation of the school will enhance school success.

The available research supports this hypothesis.[13] Schwartz identified three studies that in one way or another assessed the impact of desegregation on school success.[14] All three indicated that greater school success was a consequence of desegregation. Crain and Weisman likewise found a significant increase in school success associated with desegregation.[15]

To focus research on academic achievement is generally inappropriate because academic achievement does not have much predictive validity in important aspects of human development. We can eliminate some of the confusion over the impact of desegregation simply by using a more valid concept in evaluating that impact. In place of academic achievement, we need to substitute school success as we have defined it. Doing so will have two simultaneous effects on education research and policy.

First, it will *require* genuinely longitudinal studies. By definition, school success is a longitudinal measure requiring a number of years to develop. Second, it will solve an important measurement problem. Research in the social sciences relies on the determination of relative differences. It usually has no criteria for judging the absolute importance of those differences—their overall significance for human development.[16]

According to Crain, the methodological traditions of social science have little experience or concern with evaluating the impact of a program in relation to its costs.[17] The object of much social-science research seems to be to establish cause-and-effect relationships between variables; little thought is given to what constitutes a large or meaningful change. In other words, statistical significance and high correlation tell us little about the cost effectiveness of a program in human-resource or economic terms.[18]

Our concept of school success provides a twofold remedy for this problem. First, it asserts that the only academic achievement measures of real interest are those that indicate whether or not functional competence in basic skills has been attained. This is essentially a dichotomy—either one has mastered the skills or one has not. Thus, we avoid the many pitfalls of relative-achievement measures. Second, our concept of school success provides some units of measurement (years and institutional levels completed) that have face validity and are directly related to developmentally significant life success. We can specify a minimum level of school success as a social goal with some confidence that it makes ecological sense. Thus, we can evaluate desegregation programs on the basis of whether or not they produce a fuller realization of some quite specific school-success goals. We have concluded that the overriding principle of social habitability in the United States calls for universal secondary-school success (completion of high school with mastery of basic skills). Coupled with this is fair access to postsecondary education. In the context of what we know about the role of socioeconomic factors in shaping postsecondary-school success, a just goal would be to have no racial differences in college attendance after controlling for socioeconomic status. The problem of social class is not the major responsibility of the schools. Their responsibility is to harness social forces to meet the goals of universal secondary-school success and *racially* unbiased access to higher education. It is on these grounds that we should evaluate the academic impact of desegregation. We can eliminate much of the confusion and uncertainty surrounding studies of desegregation if we build an appropriate concept of school success into our research designs. Once we do that, research on the more purely social consequences of desegregation will fall into place, permitting us to build a valid understanding of when, how, and why desegregation works to reduce racial injustice.

Investment in Education

Although less explosive than desegregation, the issue of investment in education is nonetheless controversial. As communities and individuals struggle with the rising cost of schooling, concern grows about the outcomes of these investments. People ask whether they are getting their money's worth, and whether what they want from education is really for sale. Part of the problem, it would seem, is that we have not been clear enough about the outcomes we wish to influence. Our discussion of the meaning and origins of school success can shed some light on these questions.

The more technocratically developed the community, the less we can expect from further investment in education. An increase in investment means one thing in a setting in which the *basic* educational infrastructure is substandard and quite another when it is addressed to an already modernized setting. Investment is crucial when it provides children who were previously without formal education with teachers, books, and a respectable school building. It is marginal or irrelevant when it adds sophisticated educational technology to schools that already have teachers and books in abundance. This is a difficult lesson to learn.

The assumption in the United States (in education and other areas) has generally been that "more is always better." Jencks has shown that the addition of learning resources and educational technology does not seem to have a substantial impact on the outcomes of schooling.[19] This conclusion has been taken to mean that schools do not matter. This gross conclusion misstates the case, however. In societies in which development of the essential educational infrastructure is just beginning, investment can and does produce substantial effects.[20] Anderson put this point another way.

> Macro effects must be distinguished from micro effects. Even though all children receive identical schooling, the aggregate impact of education upon the society (in the form of productivity or citizenship) could be enormous without any individual receiving a differential benefit.[21]

As we have noted before in our analysis, the gross comparison of the "schooled" with the "unschooled" is more illuminating than any comparison of the moderately schooled and the very schooled. *Within* our society, however, the key distinctions are between those who have been deprived of an opportunity for school success and those who have had the necessary support. In terms of investment, the important differences are between students who do not have the basic equipment of schooling (teachers, books, and an adequate physical plant) and those who do. As Averch and his colleagues have found through a careful review of the evidence, once these basics are provided, further investment is nice but not critical for the important outcomes of school success.[22]

It is important that the reader understand our position on the "basics." The basic (adequate, essential) equipment of schooling consists of three things:

1. Physical facilities that are safe and allow freedom from environmental conditions that hinder learning.
2. Books, paper, pencils, and other tools that are essential to learning.
3. *Most importantly,* teachers and administrators who care about and believe in the children they are to serve.

Are massive investments beyond current levels in curricular innovation, in-service programs, or teacher training required to provide the basics? We think not. In an extensive study of learning to read as a function of instructional technique, it was found that learning to read was related not to curriculum materials or methods of instruction, but to other factors.[23] Students learned to read when they were taught by a teacher who believed in his methods and in his student's abilities to do the work. A specific theory of reading and particular curriculum materials made little difference. Combs and his colleagues came to the same conclusion with regard to teachers in general.[24] They found that good teachers do *not* hold a variety of competencies in common (such as a specific degree of content knowledge, skill in a specific teaching technique, or use of a certain set of curriculum materials) but, rather, display certain personal characteristics, regardless of teaching style.

Good teachers are those who believe that they are able and that their students are, as well. These teachers employ a variety of techniques, depending on their students' needs and backgrounds, in order to help each student achieve success. This is not to imply that content knowledge or competence in various instruction techniques is unimportant but, rather, that such competence does not distinguish good teachers from the rest of their colleagues. It is the manner in which they view themselves and their students that sets them apart from others with similar levels of knowledge and instructional skill.

Studies of reading achievement have also demonstrated the importance of administrator attitudes in promoting (or hindering) student progress.[25] The climate or feeling within a school is a direct result of the philosophy of those in charge. A belief in the ability of students to learn and of teachers to teach them, and the provision of support to meet those goals, is what seems to count, especially in those schools where student background is a hindrance to school success. Again, it is not a particular administrative organization or technique that makes a difference. It is basic philosophy and personal characteristics that appear to be important.

It would seem then that careful screening of potential teachers and administrators by colleges and universities and the use of selection measures in the hiring of staff by the schools are crucial in improving the educational climate of the schools. The answer is not huge expenditures for the newest educational gadget (technological or curricular), spectacular staff additions, or salary increases based on unorganized accumulation of college credit. What seems to make a difference in schools is the character of the staff. As the success of numerous "street academies," storefront programs, and small private schools has shown, caring and dedicated teachers and administrators can make a difference even when the other basics of schooling are lacking.[26]

What, then, are the keys to wise and effective social investment on behalf of education once the need for *adequate* facilities and equipment and *essential* staff is met? The major area of further investment should be in improving the socioeconomic lot and family support systems of the poor and struggling groups. Social policy should direct investment toward the creation and maintenance of opportunities for persons living in poor and struggling environments. This would enhance the basis for subsequent academic development of the children. The differences among communities on the

dimension of essential school success (basic skills and high-school graduation) derive from the degree to which there is a community advantage in
terms of a low proportion of families with low income or with breadwinners
who are laborers, and a low rate of unemployment.[27] The more a community consists of poor laborers subject to high rates of unemployment, the
lower its overall rate of school success. These factors accounted for between
84 and 91 percent of the variance in a series of analyses.

Offering an economic foothold can provide an important contribution
to school success. This gain far exceeds that obtained by hiring more
teachers from the affluent, educated groups, whose children already have a
high probability of academic success. The premise here, of course, is that
the contribution of the affluent, educated person to the academic success of
those not predestined to succeed is of marginal value. Once the basics have
been provided, school success is not, to any appreciable degree, the result of
the training, prior education, or income of the staff. School success comes
most directly from the community as a function of its level of
socioeconomic development or, more precisely, of the proportion of the
population who reach a habitable level of socioeconomic development.

The evidence to support this claim comes from many sources, among
them the work of Coleman, Jencks, the Council on Basic Education,
Stephens, and Dentler and Warshauer.[28] As noted earlier, 50 percent or
more of the funds allocated for special educational programs in
socioeconomically poor or struggling areas has no direct impact on the
children. Of the 50 percent or less that does, most goes to professional staff
who are themselves not indigenous to the population base they serve. A recent Rand Corporation assessment concluded that directing fiscal resources
to staff development is not a productive enterprise because it does not result
in enhanced educational development of the students.[29] The report concludes that the traditionally favorite targets for increased educational investment (for example, class size) do not pay off in improved academic attainment.

Boocock's comprehensive review of the sociology of learning reached
the same conclusion.[30] Stephens concludes that we can be much more
"relaxed" about the allocation of resources directly to teachers and concentrate those resources (as is also implied by Averch and his group) on the environmental conditions that nurture school success.[31]

Thus, a primary political question affecting schools and schooling is
whether or not people who live in poverty are given a foothold in the
socioeconomic system that supports schooling. It is *not* a question of the
provision of "learning resources" or advanced "staff development." These
things have their major impact on the profit of already established families
and groups. If we review the orientation of public-investment policy regarding schools in the more than three decades since World War II, we find

an accelerating trend toward the commitment of resources to learning materials and staff development. The primary result has been a massive profit to the affluent and educated groups through employment directly in schools or in agencies designed to provide support services or develop learning resources. Little of this investment has made any appreciable contribution to the school success of those who are in need of assistance. This is, of course, a very serious charge. But it does seem warranted. The enormous investment in education has gone and continues to go primarily to the certified teaching staff (50 percent of school budgets). This teaching staff is composed primarily of upwardly mobile lower-middle-class persons who themselves were successful enough in school to obtain the appropriate credentials.[32] Since schooling has become big business in the post–World War II era, the political decisions affecting the allocation of funds are correspondingly important. Who gets the money? Up to now, it has been mainly the children of those who already have it.

At least two conditions limit the impact of educational investment. First, resources are limited even in the most affluent communities. Second, the heart of the process of school success is not directly influenced by such investment once the essential features of a well-equipped school exist. Since these essential features are no more than books, teachers, and administrators who are competent and concerned, and a physical plant that is safe and moderately comfortable, the necessary investment is well within the reach of a modern society committed to the well-being of its children. Only communities that are not fully modern (socioeconomically) or whose power structure is founded on some pattern of social injustice (as has been the case where racial segregation and discrimination have denied adequate facilities to minority groups) have a *genuine* educational-investment problem. Our concept of school success makes this clear. Therefore, the investment problem of most U.S. communities is not really as serious as appears at first glance. The threat in most areas is to the profit of the comfortable and affluent groups that staff and control the schools. The danger is that the interests of this class will obscure the real educational needs of many communities, namely, the socioeconomic development of groups that have not yet achieved the goal of necessary school success. There is a real political issue here, and our analysis of the meaning and origins of school success highlights it.

The Role of Schools in Maintaining a Habitable Social Environment

As we pointed out in chapter 1, concern about the social habitability of U.S. schools grows. Reliable sources report sharply increased indiscipline, crime, and violence. Public-opinion surveys report growing public dissatisfaction with the deteriorating social environment of many schools. Another theme is the contention that U.S. schools are too narrowly concerned with purely academic achievement to the relative neglect of character development, moral training, and socialization to adulthood.[33]

Much of the educational establishment defends the narrow academic orientation of U.S. schools and sees social development as the proper province of family and church. The job of the schools, they say, is to foster learning, on the assumption that an acceptable set of values is brought to school from home and church. This thinking dominates the allocation of resources within our schools on a day-to-day basis.

Our concept of school success reveals the problem with this view. If our analysis has shown anything, it is that social forces provide the keys to school success. Purely academic factors are secondary and are easily provided.[34] The major problems facing our schools are social rather than strictly academic (in the narrow sense of the term). Because these problems all have some relation to the processes of school success, we can profitably note some of them.

The first problem concerns the development of a sense of personal accountability, the belief that one is responsible for one's behavior and is capable of self-determination. In his study of academic achievement,[35] Coleman found that this internal locus of control was an important correlate of achievement.[36] Wilson's study relating social relationships and ideology to competence sheds further light on this.[37] He found that accountability and internal locus of control were associated with intellectual competence (as measured by IQ).

A national study of internal locus of control reported a significant difference related to educational attainment.[38] Consider the responses to the following statement: "There is not much I can do about most of the important problems that we face today." Those with less than twelve years of schooling were more likely to agree than were those with twelve or more years, among both whites (57 percent versus 34 percent) and blacks (73 percent versus 60 percent).[39]

What do these results mean? One interpretation is, of course, that powerless people—the less intellectually competent, the less educated, and those who are denied education through discrimination and other means—accurately perceive their social position and reflect that through a psychological pattern of external locus of control. This interpretation is, of course, eminently reasonable. The converse of this view, that the reason people fail is their own ideology of external locus of control, no doubt also has some validity. Ideology can change, however, and, once changed, can alter behavior. Ideological convictions borne of the experience of social reality can become obsolete if the social realities themselves change.

The peasant or ghetto mentality tends to contradict the idea of internal locus of control. In the biographies of people who have achieved social and personal success despite growing up in socioeconomically oppressive conditions—often linked to some form of racial discrimination—one continually finds a special kind of irrationality. This irrationality lies in the belief that one does have control over one's destiny and is personally accountable despite economic deprivation and social oppression. It may be irrational to believe in internal locus of control when the social odds are against an individual or a group; but such a belief in personal power and responsibility may well be the only practical basis on which to build social success, including school success, and ultimately to overcome the odds. Where does such an irrational belief in personal power come from? Anecdotal reports (such as the biographies noted before) and more-systematic evidence suggest that it comes from demands and support for accountability in the child's immediate settings and institutions. The setting of standards of competence and accountability and the provision of the social supports necessary to meet expectations appear to be the key.

However, in many instances schools seem to discourage the development of accountability and competence in their students. Students are rarely held accountable for their actions. Rather, discipline is usually unrelated to the crime and is almost always punitive. Someone has to be blamed, and many times students are able to sidestep their own responsibility as their teachers and parents point fingers at one another. Often the school's rules themselves become the ends rather than the means. This preoccupation with rules discourages students from examining their own behavior and its consequences for themselves and others. It sets up teachers and administrators as enforcers who must make students toe the mark.

The use of the failing grade is one of the biggest obstacles to the development of student responsibility and academic competence.[40] More often than not, teachers use a grade of F as punishment for a student's socially inappropriate behavior. There is rarely an attempt to appraise the situation rationally, ascertain the student's difficulties, and develop a plan for remediation. Instead, the major task seems to be to establish blame. The student, parent, teacher, or school is at fault; and someone must step forward and acknowledge it. Because of the stigma associated with nonmastery, no one wants to be labeled as the cause. All the parties involved concentrate on ridding themselves of any responsibility and ignore the fact that the student has not mastered material that is vital to success in school. They compound this problem through social promotion, by passing functionally incompetent students along through the system until some final, unavoidable letdown occurs. Upholding high standards and helping students meet them without degrading a child who needs help is crucial, and it can be done.

Bronfenbrenner's account of education in China concluded that the egalitarian ideology of that society made it possible for the educators to insist that all children master basic skills, and to fulfill that mandate through high standards and diligent drill, without the need for punitive labels.[41] The Council for Basic Education report cited earlier noted that elementary schools that were successful in promoting mastery of reading skills among disadvantaged groups did so by means of a strong program focusing on basic skills in the context of a belief in the ability of the children to meet high standards.[42] Our own experiences in teaching and in talking with teachers also support this view that a high level of demands (standards) coupled with support is the key. Like most ideological influences, this process of demands and supports is critical in influencing outcomes as a function of the odds of success presented by the child's background—degree of support for the academic culture in the home—and ability. A review of intervention programs found that the more challenging and structured the program, the more potent its effects on the children of poor and socially oppressed parents.[43] All this becomes problematic in the academic development of children because of an increasing trend to confuse compassion with permissiveness among educators and others concerned with the moral burden of socioeconomic deprivation and racial discrimination. Kenneth Clark is one who has faced the problem forthrightly.[44] He observes that underachieving children know when they are being passed along under the guise of accepting their intellectual and cultural limitations. As Clark sees it:

> The first step in a serious job of educating youngsters in socially and racially deprived areas is to remove the rationalizations, the nonsense, the barriers, even the well-intentioned ones. . . .[45]

It is also important to note here, however, that high standards for academics and behavior should not be confused with rigidity, cruelty, or totalitarian ideology. High academic standards do not require that children be indoctrinated into a narrow value system. As Mortimer Smith, former director of the Council for Basic Education, notes, the traditional goal of schooling (literacy in word, number, and historical knowledge) remains valid. "The important thing is the human element— teachers who combine a sense of humanity and justice in dealing with young people."[46]

School organizational patterns, curriculum tinkering (at least the fine tuning of traditional programs), and particular teacher competencies in and of themselves seem to be relatively unimportant in providing the basics of schooling. What is important is the balance between high standards and support to meet those standards. Wilson found that brighter students feel that their teachers expect excellent work, whereas slow students feel that their teachers either do not care or expect poor work.[47] This is a difficult lesson to learn and, for many, a difficult pill to swallow. There is a fine line between enlightened toughness and blaming the victim. There seems to be no alternative but to walk that line. Successful parents learn to find a balance between demands and supports, and are rewarded for their efforts with competent and socially responsible children.[48] Parents encourage responsibility and independence by taking responsibility for their children and yet allowing them to be part of the decision-making process.[49] At one extreme, authoritarian parents tend to stifle the development of independence; at the other, permissive parents fail to encourage the growth of responsibility.[50] It seems increasingly difficult for Americans to chart a middle course between authoritarianism and permissiveness, each of which emphasizes one side of the equation to the neglect of the other.

All this returns to what in our view is the essential premise of U.S. society (indeed, of any Western society): Individuals must be assured of their power as individuals to control their behavior, and the society must require that they do so while offering the support necessary to enable them to accept and execute this social commission. Worsthorne sees "the rock on which a free society must always stand: the idea of man as proud and strong, master of his destiny."[51]

For the schools of the United States to do their part in affirming and sustaining this principle, they must be able to have the moral and political authority to make demands on students, and the wisdom to make those demands in ways that encourage the development of responsibility and accountibility. The impersonal and bureaucratized large schools of the United States find it hard to do this. They seem to be unable in many cases to refrain from either authoritarianism or permissiveness. One reason for this is the lack of a simple statement of the mission of schooling. It would seem that our concept of school success can provide a point of departure for defining that mission. Our analysis of the origins of school success makes it clear that once the schools are explicitly committed to the goal of universal secondary-school success, their programs can be coherently integrated around the task of establishing and maintaining the social conditions necessary to meet that goal. Fostering personal accountability and internal locus of control can facilitate that process and go far toward restoring both civility and order to the schools. The logic of combining high levels of demand and support can be a strategy of multiple advantage in this respect. This strategy can best be coupled with a reordering of the social environment of the schools to provide a better balance of collectivism versus individualism, cooperation versus competition.

U.S. schools present an odd mixture of cooperation and competition, which reveals much about our conception of human nature. This is illuminated by a series of studies by Kagan and Madsen that make clear the pervasiveness of the ideology of individual competition in American life.[52] In a series of comparisons between Mexican children and their U.S.

counterparts, they found that whereas Mexican children tend spontaneously to form cooperative groups and to work together in problem-solving situations, U.S. children (from the middle and lower classes, and including both blacks and whites) tend to compete as individuals. Such results, cutting as they do across racial and class lines, demonstrate the central role of individual competition in the ideological system of the United States. This ideology has implications for the outcome of schooling. U.S. children (and adults, for that matter) need to become more cooperative.[53]

In those areas in which the explicit purposes of schooling are clearest—principally, the transmission of knowledge and the enhancing of cognitive development—virtually all activities are organized around direct competition among the individuals within a school or classroom and, indirectly, against all individuals everywhere. In most areas touching the *implicit* goals of schooling—principally the development of character—most activities are organized around interindividual cooperation in the name of interschool competition. Although this has been noted before, relatively little has changed, despite the recommendation that interscholastic academics, academic fairs, and other devices designed to induce intraschool cooperation and interschool competition be implemented. Why? The reason, it seems, is a fundamental aspect of ideology: We view academic goals as intrinsically and inevitably individualistic and thus as best promoted through interpersonal competition. We see them as resulting directly from the personality and intelligence of the individual student. Furthermore, the success of a school is seen as represented by either the average achievement of its students or the proportion who achieve excellence. Thus, the academic goals of the school (the ones that really count) are defined by interindividual competition for a scarce resource: relative academic standing. There are virtually no superordinate academic goals.

Sherif demonstrated the power of superordinate goals, those that transcend individual interest and bind the members of a group together through common interests and purposes.[54] Such goals are the precondition for interindividual cooperation. Comparisons of cooperative and competitive tasks reinforce this view. Based on their research on the impact of task definition and group organization, Breen and Locke concluded that if the structure of the task implies cooperation, those working on the task will:

> 1) become cognitively aware that cooperation is instrumental to task success; 2) behave in a cooperative fashion; 3) develop a cathectic interest in cooperating with each other; and 4) establish norms defining cooperation as a legitimate and expected form of behavior.[55]

Some congruence of ideology and social conditions is necessary to support superordinate goals and the resulting cooperative impulse. Americans tend to see competition between individuals as a necessary (and even good) force emanating from human nature. We have developed a myth that motivation comes only from competition.[56] We cannot conceive of cooperation as the rule, rather than the exception, in important aspects of life. It seems clear that at present we as a society have an excess of competition and a deficit of cooperation.[57]

There is, nevertheless, a collective orientation in U.S. tradition. However, this orientation was linked to a series of social structures (church, neighborhood, kinship) and ideological premises (neighborliness) that have been subject to a steady process of erosion. The result has been an increasing rejection of collective identities, of social conventions, and of authority. This ideological change may be grossly summarized as a change from "do the right thing" to "do your own thing." What impact has this ideological change had on schools and schooling?

At a time when many of the support systems for schooling in the families and communities have been eroded, ideological change has reduced the legitimacy of schools and of government agencies generally.[58] The authority of schools has been weakened by reforms of various sorts. These liberating reforms have been linked historically, if not causally, to the disintegrative forces eroding the potency of many families and communities as organizers of behavior. In the midst of this social confusion, "do your own thing" has been an appealing compromise between the assertion of social authority, on the one hand, and direct conflict on the other. The schools of the United States mirror the society as a whole in this, as in many respects.

Private pockets of affluence and order—special activity groups, isolated homogeneous communities—exist within a public scene that is increasingly plagued by disorder, violation of person and property, and alienation. It seems that the old collective bonds—in both the positive and the negative sense—have largely been dissolved. In their place is an individualism unmodulated and unmediated by superordinate myths and intimate community relationships. The consequences are disconcerting. Lack of concern for the whole, expressed in some way on a day-to-day basis—if only as noblesse oblige—diminishes the quality of life. The principle of social coherence, although mythic, appears valid nonetheless. It clearly appears so for the schools of the United States, which threaten to become a social "no man's land" with no ideology of superordinate goals or collective orientation.

Embedded in all this is the ever deepening conflict between freedom and order. Some see the threat to the habitability of the U.S. environment in too much freedom at the expense of social order, whereas others see the problem in too little genuine freedom and too much social coercion. Running through all this is the need to find morally credible superordinate goals. This need may be put in slightly different language. Although the collectivist societies (most notably China) have achieved a high level of social cohesion and morale, they have done so at the cost of personal freedom. In a poor society with a high ratio of population to socioeconomic resources, the tradeoff of freedom for cohesion and substantial socioeconomic guarantees is understandable. But for affluent societies (most notably the United States) such a tradeoff would be a tragedy.

Our characteristic revulsion toward authoritarianism is well justified. However, the forces of social disintegration that are plaguing many parts of U.S. society make it essential that we find ways to preserve essential liberty while generating the social cohesion, morale, and order that collectivist systems engender. Perhaps the major question for public policy is whether or not there is a moral equivalent to totalitarianism. In many ways, this is the central question affecting—or, one might say, *afflicting*—the Western republics. Is it possible to give the schools the power they need to change the destiny of those who are doomed to academic failure and socioeconomic marginality, while maintaining the essential humanism of a pluralist republic?

William James asked for a "moral equivalent to war." We are still looking for one, for some way to get the benefits of collective goals without the costs. The American answer has been to substitute affluence for commitment, to try to buy social change. The results have been disappointing.[59]

Human nature is no more individualistic than it is collective, no more competitive than it is cooperative.[60] It contains the potential for each of these attributes. It is a series of potentials that culturally defined settings realize in varying degrees. There is evidence that "do your own thing" can be replaced with "do the right thing," that we can establish a collective and cooperative pattern of ideology and behavior. The key is the skillful use of superordinate goals. The concept of school success advanced in our analysis can provide the focal point for such a program of superordinate goals. One can easily imagine the fruitful consequences of organizing our schools around the goal of universal secondary-school success, and of doing so in the context of small schools.

Classes can be "graded" on the basis of their collective success in mastering basic skills and in promoting the involvement of those who are natural candidates for alienation. Interpersonal competition would be eliminated as a motivator for academic achievement, to be replaced by intrapersonal competition with interpersonal support. Students would be encouraged to help each other learn, rather than to compete against each other for grades. Nonmastery would mean that a student would have to keep trying (maybe with extra help) until he achieved mastery, but it would not brand him as a failure. And certainly no student would ever be passed along without first having mastered the skills needed for success.

Interscholastic contests in academic competence would join interscholastic athletics. Intramural academics, like their parallel in intramural athletics, would be designed to develop universal fitness and provide an opportunity for personal challenge and testing. Academic achievement would be put in its proper place as only one aspect of schooling—one that, along with others, contributes to the superordinate goal of cooperation and concern for the common good. By introducing our concept of school success as the focal point for superordinate goals, we would anticipate an increase in cooperative behavior and ideology that would have many beneficial side effects on schools as contexts for social development: successful schools and competent students.

Notes

1. A. Holden, *The Bus Stops Here: A Study of School Desegregation in Three Cities* (New York: Agathon Press, 1974); N. St. John, *School Desegregation Outcomes for Children* (New York: John Wiley and Sons, 1975).

2. A. Summers, "Angels in Purgatory: Los Angeles Awaits Two Decisions on Mandatory Busing for Desegregation," *Phi Delta Kappan* 60 (1979):718-722.

3. Ibid.

4. R. Crain, "Why Academic Research Fails to Be Useful," *School Review* 84 (1976):337-351.

5. H. Proshansky, "Environmental Ecology and the Real World," *American Psychologist* 31 (1976):303-310; J. Garbarino and U. Bronfenbrenner, *Research on Parent-Child Relations and Social Policy: How to Proceed,* Boys Town Center for the Study of Youth Development, Working Paper Series no. 1, 1977.

6. B. Commoner, *The Closing Circle: Nature, Man and Technology* (New York: Alfred P. Knopf and Company, 1971).

7. Crain, "Academic Research."

8. Ibid., p. 337.

9. Crain, "Academic Research"; St. John, *School Desegregation Outcomes.*

10. C. Jencks, *Inequality: A reassessment of the Effect of Family and Schooling in America* (New York: Basic Books, 1972).

11. St. John, *School Desegregation Outcomes.*

12. Crain, "Academic Research."

13. A. Schwartz, "Social Science Evidence and the Objectives of School Desegregation," School of Education, University of Southern California, Los Angeles, 1975.

14. Ibid.

15. R. Crain and C. Wiseman, *Discrimination Personality and Achievement* (New York: Seminar Press, 1972).

16. Garbarino and Bronfenbrenner, *Research and Social Policy.*

17. Crain, "Academic Research."

18. Ibid.

19. Jencks, *Inequality.*

20. J. Farrell et al., "Review Symposium: Jencks and Inequality," *Comparative Educational Review* 18 (1974):430–439.

21. C. Anderson, "A Skeptical Note on Education and Mobility," in *Education, Economy and Society: A Reader in the Sociology of Education,* ed. A. Halsey, J. Floud, and C. Anderson (New York: Free Press, 1961).

22. H. Averch et al., *How Effective Is Schooling? A Critical Review of Research* (Englewood Cliffs, N.J.: Educational Technology Publications, 1974).

23. G. Bond and R. Dykstra, "The Cooperative Research Program in First-Grade Reading Instruction," *Reading Research Quarterly* 2 (1967):5–141.

24. A. Combs et al., *The Professional Education of Teachers* (Boston: Allyn and Bacon, 1974).

25. G. Weber, "Inner-City Children Can be Taught to Read: Four Successful Schools," (Council for Basic Education, Occasional Papers: No. 18, 1971).

26. For examples, D. Henry, "Love and Discipline Spawn Education in Midst of Despair," *New York Times,* 16 November 1980, "Education" section, p. 14.

27. R. Dentler and M. Warshauer, U.S. Department of Health, Education and Welfare, Center for Urban Education, *Big City Dropouts and Illiterates* (Washington, D.C.: U.S. Government Printing Office, 1964).

28. J. Coleman et al., *Equality of Educational Opportunity* (Washington, D.C.: U.S. Government Printing Office, 1966); Jencks, *Inequality;* Council for Basic Education, "Schools Do Make a Difference" (New York: Council for Basic Education, 1967); J. Stephens, *The Process of Schooling: A Psychological Examination* (New York: Holt, Rinehart and Winston, 1967); Dentler and Warshauer, *Big City Dropouts.*

29. Averch, *How Effective Is Schooling?*

30. S. Boocock, *An Introduction to the Sociology of Learning* (Boston: Houghton Mifflin, 1972).

31. Stephens, *The Process of Schooling.*

32. C. Silberman, *Crisis in the Classroom: The Remaking of American Education* (New York: Random House, 1970).

33. U. Bronfenbrenner, *Two Worlds of Childhood: U.S. and U.S.S.R.* (New York: Russell Sage Foundation, 1970).

34. Stephens, *The Process of Schooling.*

35. Coleman, *Equality of Educational Opportunity.*

36. J. Rotter, "Generalized Expectancies for Internal Versus External Control of Reinforcement," *Psychological Monographs: General and Applied* 80 (1966):1–28.

37. A. Wilson, "Sociological Perspectives on the Development of Academic Competence in Urban Areas," in *Urban Education in the 70's: Reflections and a Look Ahead,* ed. A. Passow (New York: Columbia University, Teacher's College Press, 1971).

38. U.S. Department of Health, Education and Welfare, *Toward a Social Report* (Washington, D.C.: U.S. Government Printing Office, 1969).

39. Ibid.

40. C. Johnson, "Secondary Schools and Student Responsibility," *Phi Delta Kappan* 60 (1978):338–341.

41. U. Bronfenbrenner, in *Childhood in China* ed. W. Kessen et al. (New Haven, Conn.: Yale University Press, 1975).

42. Council for Basic Education, "Schools Do Make a Difference."

43. U. Bronfenbrenner, *Is Early Intervention Effective?* (Washington, D.C.: U.S. Department of Health, Education and Welfare, 1974).

44. K. Clark, "Education in the Ghetto: A Human Concern," in *Urban Education in the 70's,* ed. A. Passow.

45. Ibid., p. 99.

46. M. Smith, *"CBE Views the Alternatives,"* in *Alternative Education: A Sourcebook for Parents, Teachers and Administrators,* ed. Mario Fantini (Garden City, N.Y.: Anchor Books, 1976), p. 49.

47. Wilson, "Academic Competence."

48. D. Baumrind, "Some Thoughts About Childrearing," in *Influences on Human Development,* ed. U. Bronfenbrenner and M. Mahoney (Chicago: Dryden Press, 1975); Bronfenbrenner, *Two Worlds of Childhood.*

49. B. Rosen and R. D'Andrade, "The Psycho-Social Origins of Achievement Motivation," *Sociometry* 22 (1959):185–217.

50. G. Elder, "Structural Variations in the Child-Rearing Relationship," Sociometry, 25 (1962):241–262.

51. P. Worsthorne, "A Universe of Hospital Patients," *Harper's,* November 1975, pp. 34–38.

52. S. Kagan and M. Madsen, "Experimental Analysis of Cooperation and Competition of Anglo American and Mexican Children," *Developmental Psychology* 6 (1972):49–59.

53. J. Brophy, *Child Development and Socialization* (Chicago: Science Research Associates, 1977).

54. M. Sherif, "Superordinate Goals in the Reduction of Intergroup Conflict," *American Journal of Sociology* 63 (1958):349–356.

55. P. Breen and E. Locke, *Task Experience as a Source of Attitudes* (Homewood, Ill.: Dorsey Press, 1964).

57. U. Bronfenbrenner, *Two Worlds of Childhood.*

58. U. Bronfenbrenner, "The Origins of Alienation," in *Influences on Human Development,* ed. Bronfenbrenner and Mahoney.

59. Bronfenbrenner, "The Origins of Alienation"; J. Coleman et al., *Youth: Transition to Adulthood* (Chicago: University of Chicago Press, 1974).

60. J. Garbarino, "The Issue is Human Quality: In Praise of Children," *Children and Youth Services Review* 1 (1979):353–377.

Index

Abramson, P., 21
Academic ability, 59. *See also* Cognitive
  ability
Academic Achievement, 11-12, 56, 60, 62,
  76, 92, 94, 98, 147-148; and life success,
  36
Academic competence, 72
Academic culture, 68, 70-79, 125; in Great
  Britain, 74; support for, 74, 78
Academic development, 84
Academic excellence, 32-33, 34; and social
  class, 33-36. *See also* Academic achieve-
  ment
Academic failure: and juvenile deliquency,
  42-43; and school size, 43; and social
  class, 42
Academic growth, 5
Achievement scores, 77
Adams High School, 5-6, 8
Adams, W., 49
Adler, J., 21
Affirmative action, 54
Africa, 126
Albee, G., 48
Alexander, K., 127, 140
Alienation, 115, 117, 118
Aliens, 54, 60
Almond, G., 41, 49-50
Alternative schools, 3, 79. *See also* Educa-
  tional innovation
American Council of Education, 135
American Dream, 92
Anderson, A., 41, 64
Anderson, C., 49-50, 64, 66, 104-105,
  141-143, 150, 162
Armstrong, C., 62, 66
Aronowitz, S., 102, 106
Atlanta, summer achievement, 73
Authoritarianism, 118
Averch, H., 20, 65, 89, 122, 150-152, 162

Baird, L., 104, 113, 121
Baker, K., 21, 22
Ban, J., 22
Barker, D., 48
Barker, R., 23, 43, 50, 103-105, 112-115,
  121-122
Basic skills, 68-69, 91
Baumrind, D., 163
Becerra, R., 48
Bee, H., 49
Berger, M., 86
Blyth, D., 115, 122-123

Bond, G., 162
Boocock, S., 48, 88-89, 152, 162
Borow, H., 49-51
Boudon, R., 51
Bowles, S., 59, 66
Bradley, R., 87
Bradley, W., 141
Breckinridge, S., 48
Breen, P., 158, 163
Brice, R., 88
Brody, E., 64
Brody, N., 64
Broman, S., 69, 86
Bronfenbrenner, U., 14, 21-23, 26, 28, 47,
  49, 65, 81, 87, 89, 98, 105, 118, 120,
  122-123, 143, 156, 161-164
Brooks, K., 5, 20
Broom, L., 49
Brophy, J., 163
Brown, B., 65
Budig, G., 142
Burkhead, J., 122
Burns, M., 121
Bush, D., 115, 122-123
Butler, J., 142
Buxton, C., 117, 123

Caldwell, B., 87
Cambridge, 134
Campbell, A., 45, 51
Caplan, G., 111, 120, 123
Carew, J., 71-72, 86-87
Carnegie Foundation, 6
Cather, W., 126, 140
Chase, J., 8, 21
Chicanos, 93
Chickering, A., 137, 142
Child maltreatment, 108
Children out of school, 57-58, 84-85;
  Minnesota, 57; Mississippi,
  57
Children's Defense Fund, 56-60, 65-66,
  84-85, 89, 120
Christensen, S., 130, 141
Churchill, W., 117
Ciminillo, L., 22
Cisin, I., 65
Citizenship, 119
City University of New York, 128
Clark, B., 116, 122
Clark, K., 44, 50, 156, 163
Climate, 110
Cochran, M., 89

165

About the Authors

James Garbarino is associate professor of human development at The Pennsylvania State University and was a Fellow and director of the Maltreatment of Youth Project at the Boys Town Center for the Study of Youth Development. He received the Ph.D. in human development and family studies from Cornell University in 1973. Dr. Garbarino's research includes the study of the human ecology of abusive families. He is the author of numerous articles and of two other books, *Protecting Children From Abuse and Neglect: Creating and Maintaining Family Support Systems* and *Understanding Abusive Families*. In 1975 he was named a Spencer Fellow by the National Academy of Education; in 1979 he won a Mitchell Prize from the Woodlands Conference on Growth Policy for his paper, "The Issue Is Human Quality: In Praise of Children;" and in 1981 he was named a National Fellow by the W.K. Kellogg Foundation.

C. Elliott Asp is a doctoral student in human development and family studies at The Pennsylvania State University. He has worked with youth in a number of capacities, including five years as a junior-high-school teacher. He was a staff associate with the Biological Sciences Curriculum Study, where he helped develop curriculum materials for use with middle-school/junior-high-school students and the mentally handicapped both at the elementary and the secondary levels. Mr. Asp holds the B.A. in biology from the University of Colorado at Boulder and received the M.A. in education from the University of Northern Colorado.